SMART EXIT™

SMART EXIT™

STEER YOUR BUSINESS TO SUCCESS

JOHN E. ANDERSON

AMERICA PUBLISHING COMPANY
Longview, Washington and North Bend, Oregon

Copyright

Library of Congress Cataloging-in-Publication Data

Author – Anderson, John E.

Title – Smart Exit   Sub-Title – Steer Your Business To Success   Includes index.

Print Version – ISBN # 978-1-58600-000-4
eBook Version – ISBN # 978-1-58600-001-1

Published by America Publishing Company, 67539 East Bay Road, North Bend, Oregon 97459 • 800-249-1622
Printed in the United States of America

Contents

Smart Exit™

Steer Your Business To Success

Plan Yours Now!

A practical guide for growing the value of your business,

identifying and mentoring a successor,

selling the business to the new leader,

and making a Smart Exit™.

Smart Exit™ is intended for firms with 3 to 100 employees,

revenue of $100,000 to $100 million.

By John E. Anderson,

MS, Management

Preface

It was the day the area's largest logging firm laid off most of their employees pulling their equipment out of the forests. That day, I happened to call and introduce myself to David Goodroe, executive director of the Economic Development Center of Wahkiakum County, Washington. It was December 2009. David explained that 10% of the jobs in the county had just ended.

Be Cause Business was hired to produce a business fair to stimulate a spark of hope in the business community. We worked with David, local business leaders and brought in seven speakers, including a member of the Federal Reserve, Sandra Suran, Marketing Ninja Jerry Fletcher, Wahkiakum business leader Richard Erickson and others. There were business exercises, collaboration, and new ideas that day at Norse Hall on Puget Island in February 2010.

Business Navigation 101

Later in 2010 and following years, I offered my Business Navigation 101 classes streaming online and in Pacific Northwest communities including Longview, Coos Bay, Oregon City and

Wahkiakum County. I created an online platform so business owners could participate on their own schedule. There were further classes on strategic planning, teleconferenced from the Small Business Development Center at Southwestern Oregon Community College from Coos Bay to the Brookings campus. A "Right Person, Right Job" course was developed based upon firms using the Core Values Index assessment to have high performing teams improve effectiveness, efficiency, and profit.

I presented one-hour Smart Exit™ panel talks with attorneys and accountants backed by insurance and commercial real estate brokers at the Bay Area Chamber of Commerce, Umpqua Banks in Vancouver and Roseburg and various business gatherings in Portland, Vancouver, and Longview. Other Smart Exit™ and Strategic Planning talks were presented at the Castle Rock Washington Chamber and Washington's Cowlitz County Small Business Development Center.

"Smart Exit™ Strategic Planning"

In October – November 2015, I produced a "Smart Exit™ Strategic Planning" course in a five-session, 10-hour program with eight guest speakers in Vancouver. These programs were video recorded and coursework developed.

My research, client experiences, and management studies gave rise to the course workbooks and now have gradually coalesced into this book.

Acknowledgments

My clients, my colleagues at the Institute of Management

Consultants, the Be Cause Business Team and of course my wife Kate have all contributed greatly to my being able to write this book. My son, Esana Anderson has worked closely with me over the last few years and his ideas and critiques have influenced what a book should be in 2016.

Alexis Mason, Shanna Woeller, Sandy Crowell, Wahai Brad Gray and many other author friends have over the years contributed large and small to encourage me forward in the process. It was Janice Aday, however, who insisted we could get this book edited and finished by June 1st, 2016 and may be most responsible for the final single-handed effort to edit the manuscript to its core message.

Thank you, Janice, and to the many other colleagues and clients who have helped to make this book possible. I am truly grateful and appreciative!

The Author

John E. Anderson has founded five companies, two of which he sold. John is president/CEO at the management consultancy Be Cause Business Resources, Inc., specialists in small business value optimization, smooth leadership succession and successful owner exit. He's a regular contributor to business journals, speaks to trade associations, teaches operations management at the university level and is president of the Institute of Management Consultants for Oregon and Washington.

He was born in Syracuse, New York. He graduated from Jersey Preparatory School in 1964 and from Monmouth College in 1967 with an Associate of Arts majoring in English. In 1969 John earned a Bachelor of Arts degree in philosophy at Bloomfield College, Bloomfield New Jersey.

Newspaper/Trade Paper Editor

After six months reporting and editing at two weekly papers – the Newark Record and Bellevue Times – John was a staff writer at daily Passaic-Clifton Herald News while attending Bloomfield College. Upon graduation, John became a writer and editor at

Fairchild Publishing, New York, at the daily trade paper, "Home Furnishings Daily," from 1969 to 1971.

Between 1969 and 1972, John completed a full curriculum of philosophy and anthropology graduate courses at the New School for Social Research in New York, studying with philosophers Hannah Arendt, Hans Jonas, Aaron Gurvitch and the anthropologist Stanley Diamond.

Founding & Selling Ventures

John resigned from Fairchild, traveled and then with a friend, Steven Finkelstein, founded and operated Unison Natural Foods in Middletown, New York during 1971 and 1972. He later worked with his family in Anderson Travel Agency.

In 1976, John founded America Publishing Company in Florida specializing in tourism development. During the following 10 years, he produced 100+ color brochures, began a monthly cultural magazine, "Space Coast News," and a wholesale inbound tour operation, Sunny Tours. Sunny Tours was a reception tour operator working with Amtrak and 100-passenger ultra yachts on the Intercoastal Waterway stopping at the Kennedy Space Center. John marketed the first cruise ship from Port Canaveral and he was awarded contracts to operate a Florida Greyhound Bus Station and Western Union Agency. John sold two businesses during this time: the Space Coast News and the Western Union Agency.

Between 1986 and 1989, John studied accounting and finance, passed the H&R Block tax course, and health/life insurance license examinations. He worked with an insurance agency in Florida and wrote business plans for clients' marketing, finance and retirement. Between 1989 and 2001, John moved to Oregon, operated an art gallery and published greeting card lines for 12+ artists which he marketed with the gift lines of many artisans to 1,000 independent retail stores coast-to-coast.

Int'l Consulting Group & Masters Degree

From 2001 to 2005, John worked for an international management consulting firm, appraising hundreds of businesses and earning a Master of Science degree in management from Antioch University in Seattle with two professional certifications in change management. John founded Be Cause Business Resources in 2003 after a study of coaching and large system facilitation.

He's been a member of Toastmasters International Early Words club in Longview, Washington since 2009. He served as Public Relations Officer in 2014 – 2015 for Oregon and SW Washington, achieving the highest honor of Distinguished Toastmaster in 2015. At Early Words, he's a past president and has held various vice-president roles. John has been a professional member of the Institute of Management Consultants since 2007, and served as membership chair on the Oregon – SW Washington board for three years and as president from 2016 to the present. He received national recognition from IMC for doubling chapter membership. John facilitated the monthly non-profit speakers' series at the Thursday Member Focus, Vancouver 2013-2016. At the Carson College of Business, Washington State University-Vancouver, John volunteered as a mentor to students and their business clients in the Business Growth Mentor and Analysis

Program from 2015-2017. He taught management operations as an adjunct professor in 2017.

John has developed a broad range of services for Be Cause Business clients in Oregon, Washington, California, and other states with a focus upon organization optimization, staff succession with leadership transition and successful owner/ partner exit.

Introduction

Change, Catharsis, and Metamorphosis

There are beginnings and there are endings. Change is exciting and disruptive. When we are ripped asunder by change, it is called trauma. Years can be needed for recovery. When we can merge with the change, when we "become" the change, it is called birth, growth, development, and it is sought after and good. This is a book about "being" the change.

When our ideas work, we love the process of change and we want it to last forever. When complexity overwhelms us, we become dizzy, doubtful and demand that it STOP!

In the following pages, I'm going to share with you fundamentals of small business management for the purpose of preparing for a successful exit. I propose that these concepts and principles can be fashioned to become a personalized guidance system for you, individually and for your firm.

Metamorphosis requires letting go of the old in favor of the new. This can require discontinuing marginal business services and products while exploring new offerings and updating your brand.

Giving up established habits, even when they don't serve us, can be confronting. We need time and resources to create a better future. We must trust that by becoming "empty," what we will receive will be a real improvement over what we have had.

Early preparation for succession involves optimizing the venture, developing staff talent, and creating a strategy for the owner's exit. This work improves stability in the leaders' lives, their families and in their communities.

While business owners age 50 and older face the most immediate need for planning, all organization managers of any age, for any size venture, both for-profit and non-profit, should be developing their staff and preparing for succession. Employees *and* owners are inevitably replaced by new ones. Healthy organizations *require* change and growth.

Businesses with similar numbers of employees, annual revenue, and within the same industry share many succession and exit issues. At the same time, each venture and group has its own unique circumstances that must be addressed to ensure healthy succession.

Building a stronger business, with increased customer demand and revenue, enables firms to hire staff and managers. The staff must be shown how to scale volume up *and* down, for obvious reasons. This is a fundamental concern in optimizing an organization: Teach your staff to "steer" the venture.

Attracting new talent, documenting staff training and job position progression are other important "steering" mechanisms that will enable managers to grow, maintain or shrink operations to fit customer demand, so the owner, top management and officers can be gradually less involved in daily operations.

Optimization, Succession, and Exit Stories

Real-life stories herein are examples of what happens in the optimization and succession process. Names of individuals and their organizations have been changed.

A valued colleague of mine says all business problems are people problems. After reading the stories I think you will agree. The mindset and tools we choose to use greatly influence our effectiveness and ability to innovate solutions. Those tools and world-views are created by people.

We must remain open to new ideas and approaches while not careening wildly from one approach to another. That balance between openness and stick-to-it-iveness is crucial to our ability to adapt and succeed.

A few of the stories have recorded interviews to give you a more detailed accounting of the actions and mindsets of executives and small business owners who think ahead and, by doing so, benefit their customers and themselves. View video interviews at BeCauseBusiness.com/conversations

All organizations begin with an idea, an entrepreneurial insight shared from one person to another. Some ideas take root and grow; some don't. Some ventures last decades; some last weeks or months.

There are tens of thousands of one- and two-person businesses throughout the world. Many new ventures are begun and operated by a person who received specialized training and worked for a large organization where they mastered their trade. Then they were laid off or retired. At some point, they realized they were in possession of skills and abilities that had value. Perhaps they considered another job, then weighed a new job with a new boss and decided their skills could enable them to start their own business. In collaboration with a friend or family member, or on their own, they set out and established a new enterprise.

Staying small is crucial for many of these folks because while they have some expertise they can market, they often have little business, management, or organizational skill. They're usually lacking in bookkeeping ability or just have no patience for it. They muddle through or hire a bookkeeper and tax preparer to keep them in conformity with the law.

With perspective, we see that projects and businesses have a beginning, development, and conclusion. With this perspective, we can prepare early for the conclusion to be successful. We earn money from operating a business. If executed properly, we can get a second, and possibly greater income by successfully transferring that business rather than just ending it carelessly.

Map Your Future!

My dad, Stanley Anderson, retired from the federal government at age 55 and immediately opened a small business with my mom, Dorothy. Friends in his office had retired before him. He watched as they became lethargic, frequently had heart attacks and died within a year or two. He had already survived a heart attack, a serious auto accident and the death of his best friend. Dad was determined that wouldn't happen to him! At 17, I was impressed by his "I can do this" attitude, and I guess it has influenced me ever since. Over the next 20+ years, I worked on and off with my folks in their business, began a number of my own businesses and always wished I could contribute more to their enterprise and their dreams.

My first full-time jobs were as a newspaper reporter, first at a weekly paper, followed by a daily, and then at an international trade paper in Manhattan. I received a bachelor's degree and did several years of graduate study in philosophy. Between the ages of 19 to 24, I observed, reflected upon and wrote about life as a reporter and philosophy student before deciding I'd rather be the "actor," the dynamic participant in the drama, than a passive witness reporting from the sidelines. I dedicate Smart Exit™ to all entrepreneurs, who, like my folks, have struck out with a dream to energize their lives and serve the customers they long to assist.

This book is a map to guide you to improving how you serve in your business. Your job as an entrepreneur, I say, is to mentor employees to assist you. Later, turn the business over to them, selling it to them, so you can go on to your next project. I offer this to you with my best wishes and good luck!

Footnotes

All footnotes and resource updates will made periodically on our website to keep up to date with website addresses which are subject to change. I am centralizing all notes, footnotes and resource links at: Smart-Exit.com/notes

I have produced entrepreneur curricula offered online and in person at business groups such as Small Business Development Centers (SBDC), Economic Development Councils (EDC), Chambers of Commerce and colleges. Smart Exit course material has been developed into the *Smart Exit Companion Workbook*. Watch Smart-Exit.com and BeCauseBusiness.com for news.

Part I

Part I - Why Plan Your Exit Now?

Try on a new mind-set.

The intention of this book is to give you first a glimpse, then an understanding and finally an appreciation for how a firm's value might be increased, then the venture be prepared and a successful ownership transfer be completed.

Most entrepreneurs see themselves first and foremost as a craftsman in their industry: a physician, carpenter, dentist, chef, attorney, machinist, chiropractor. We suggest that yes, you do have that expertise but as the owner of the business you are the CEO of a medical practice, construction company, dental practice, restaurant, law firm, manufacturer, health clinic.

We want to encourage you to think more of your company responsibilities and less of the industry expertise from this point forward. As owner of the company you now employ expert physicians, carpenters, etc. and it's *their* job to master and maintain their industry expertise. It's now your fundamental responsibility to operate a successful firm employing them.

In changing mind sets from craftsman to business owner successfully, tricky waters may need to be navigated to securely deposit the fruits of your many years of labor into a tax-protected retirement account.

We recommend a team approach to address the variety of important topics needed for resolution for successful transfer in a timely manner. There are different types of experts who have specialty education, training and experience to augment the legal and financial transfer work of attorneys and accountants.

These experts range from your insurance agent and investment advisor to specialist teams for mergers/acquisitions, security broker/market makers, commercial real estate brokers and business brokers. We'll explain some of these transfer options and the experts who facilitate them in the following pages.

I

CHAPTER 1 - THE DANCE AND THE LEADER OF THE ORGANIZATION

———————

"When a man does not know which harbor he is heading for, no wind is the right wind." Seneca *(Roman philosopher)*

You and your organization have become locked in an exquisite dance. Yet, like most of the exquisite, excitement and drama mask danger. That mix of drama and danger may add to your fascination.

Starting and staying in business has always been a gamble. You might strike it *really* big or strike out! It might be worse to succeed marginally, to survive but not thrive. You *have* succeeded and have beaten the odds. Have you become comfortable and unconscious?

The good news is advancements in technology, communications and economics may *now* allow you to realize your lifelong dreams.

The Time is Now!

It's time to prepare your Smart Exit™ regardless of your age, or how many years you've been in business. The time is now to prepare for your successful exit from your current organization. You've got to prepare or you may lose most of the business value you've created and your organization may falter and fail before you leave, or shortly thereafter.

There is a chance to avoid calamity, but you and your organization will need to make changes to achieve the greater success you *really* desire. Depending on your situation, this could be next year or 10 years from now. But begin now to prepare the conclusion of your involvement with the firm. And with a handsome addition to your investment portfolio.

Your ability to create and influence circumstances in the world is greater now than at any prior time in history. Of course, there are still great obstacles, daunting challenges, and work, work, work in various forms, but the fact remains that we, as individuals organizing into teams, can achieve ambitious projects to a far greater degree than at any time since the beginning of civilization.

Science is now telling us our brains are easier to mold and optimize than many other parts of the physical body. Therefore, our thoughts, our communication, and collaboration abilities can enable us to organize successful efforts like never before.

It's been your faith in yourself and your unique business idea that has kept your hope alive for years, through the good times and perhaps some very bad times. You *can* achieve the goals you have set. Congratulations. Read on: The tools and methods that will advance you on the journey are before you here.

Racing the Clock

Succession and exit are of crucial concern for you, other current leaders in your firm, and those who will follow.

For many leaders, succession and exit are in the future, years from now, so why worry about that today? For these executives, and really any active leader, I say, "Congratulations!" Amid the layoffs, liquidations, closures and foreclosures which sweep the economy, your venture is still standing. WOW, what an accomplishment!

But your challenges are not over. Having survived, you are *now facing a new hurdle in your career.*

Can you identify the next leader of your group who, with your mentoring, can take your organization to the next level? Succession takes time and sometimes more than one try. If you think succession planning and your ultimate exit are years away, that's great because you probably need every one of those years to do it right. There's more to succession than many anticipate.

You've brought the company this far; look around and ask yourself who can take it further. As the leader, it's your responsibility to select and nurture the next generation of leadership.

Regardless of whether you are considering your succession and exit this year or in 5, 10, or 15 years, *now is the time to begin preparation.*

If you read that and thought to yourself, "Oh, but I have a plan", consider when your plan was last reviewed and updated. Most small organizations have exit plans like they have business plans, strategy, and budgets; they are "mental" plans, not written down intelligently so their attorney, accountant and family members could understand and implement them.

Attorneys suggest including dissolution provisions in partnership and corporation agreements when firms are first begun. They recommend succession and exit options from the very beginning for good reason. It's of great importance to have and maintain succession, transfer and exit plans for you and your key employees. Cross-training and key person insurance are part of a good plan, but there are a number of key elements which work together to improve your firm's stability and sustainability. You and several other employees, I am sure, are very important to your firm in maintaining major client, banking, and financial relationships.

It's one thing for a leader to be absent a few days or a week. If one or several of you were absent for an extended period, would your operation be endangered?

It's good to review and improve the abilities of multiple persons to step into different leadership roles for at least two reasons:

- To prepare for the eventuality of someone important being unavailable and,

- To stimulate change and innovation when a department or branch has become stale, as they all do.

Given our current technological, social and competitive

environments, change is rarely comfortable. But like it or not, it's good for us and it's good for the organization.

Entrepreneurs don't or can't stop being entrepreneurial. They (or we) are frequently serial entrepreneurs. Once a person is successful in beginning, operating and concluding a venture, it's hard not to see even better opportunities and want to do it again, only better.

It's fun. It's exciting. It's dynamic, challenging and rewarding. It can also be terrifying when a business goes sideways fast and crashes. Let's avoid crashing! Let's routinely do staff development. Let's identify and mentor our future leaders. There will always be surprises but we can minimize loss by preparing in advance.

Steps to Business Transfer Success

Our 4-step method for successful small business transfer is:

1. **Deliver Customer Delight.** Grow an efficient venture that delights your customers.

2. **Teach Staff to Steer.** Train and develop your staff to operate and steer the business, based upon written policies and procedures. Identify a new leader. Support leader candidates – who wants it most?

3. **Implement Financial and Management Controls.** Monitor company performance, keeping close reins as staff and the new leader practice with less of your direct involvement.

4. **Make Your Smart Exit.™** Smoothly and gracefully, transfer responsibilities, leadership, and ownership and make a Smart

Exit™ to go on to your next opportunities, enterprises or retirement.

The following lists the tools and machinery needed to achieve these steps in the four key areas of 1) Reliable Accounting; 2) Strategic Planning; 3) Business Valuation; 4) Communication.

1. Reliable Accounting

- Maintain your accounting with software like QuickBooks and possibly a point-of-sale system .

- Post deposits and payments and reconcile to your bank frequently so your checkbook balances are fully accurate. The frequency will be a function of the volume of transactions and the level of cushion in the bank.

- Categorize transactions so your financial statements are correct and informative.

2. Strategic Planning

- Conduct scenario planning with projections into the next year or beyond, based upon your history.

- Write lists of the ideas to improve and sustain your business and manage these initiatives with project management methods.

- Write strategies and tactics for how to implement the lists of improvements. Clarify the value proposition you offer. Explain why customers want to do business with you. Determine how you will steadily improve your customer service.

3. Business Valuation

- Maintain spreadsheets of your assets, liabilities and obligations for an understanding of routine commitments you must fulfill to remain in business.

- Establish for yourself and stockholders the value of the enterprise. Do this yearly.

4. Communication

- In all that your firm says and does, communicate the vision, mission, purpose, your culture, your brand and the "why" of what you do.

- Engage and develop a team of supporters, stakeholders, customers and employees to build your fulfillment process.

- Develop win/win written agreements with vendors, employees, and stockholders to fulfill your promise to customers. Build trust and confidence in all your relationships.

Does this sound like a big project? It is. We'll show you how you can learn, practice and perfect your methods, improve your business value and transfer leadership in the coming pages.

Four Organizational Risks

It may be difficult to accept that **YOU** represent several risks to the ongoing success of your organization. You could drop dead, be diagnosed with a terminal illness, or win the lottery and no longer be interested in or care about your business. Things like this can and do shut businesses down every day.

Here are a few questions to ponder.

- If you were incapacitated or dead, what would your family have to do to close your venture and liquidate assets?

- Is your organization stable enough to survive if you have a personal calamity?

- How would your family and business recover and carry on successfully?

Your early death or disability would be a "train wreck" for your family. If your business functions successfully with or without your daily involvement, your death will still be devastating to your family, but less so for the business.

All organizations face four primary risks: "the truck, the diagnosis, the lottery and exhaustion." You've navigated these waters well so far, but the currents in this next section can be trickier than what's come before. You must explicitly deal with these possible scenarios or they can wipe out all you've worked to achieve.

1. THE TRUCK

"The Truck" is some unexpected event that radically changes your involvement in your business. It could be an accident, a stroke or heart attack. One day you're fine and the next minute you are out with two broken legs, a broken back, head trauma or dead. Think major auto collision, criminal attack, tornado, volcano, tsunami, or a raging fire at your office or home.

Generally, we just don't see the "truck" coming. If we have

substantial resources available, it can help. Sometimes resources don't matter and it's a struggle for those left behind to move forward.

2. THE DIAGNOSIS

"The Diagnosis" is a surprise that, while there is nothing physically noticeable, there is some significant change coming in your business or personal future SOON. It could be your major vendor dropping you, or a change in government regulations making your service obsolete.

One day things are fine, as perhaps they've been for years, and the next day you learn *big* change is coming. Your wife or business partner tells you they are done, it's over, she or he is leaving in 60 days. Or you are a Ford dealer and Ford Motor Company notifies you that your contract has been terminated effective the end of the month or year. All is operationally the same, but some big change is headed your way.

It could be a phone call after a routine medical exam in which you learn one of the many routine tests you took is positive for a disease. Suddenly the words you hear from your doctor change your priorities and your life in a moment's time. You still look fine, but you know, everything is going to be different from here on out. No one around you knows or suspects what that phone call means. You're holding the phone and wondering what to do next.

3. THE LOTTERY

Winning the lottery may be wonderful for the individual winner but terrible for the people who have depended on the lottery winner. You, the owner or a key employee, wins the lottery and life is again completely different once the news is received. Life's priorities suddenly and dramatically shift. You hear of lottery winners in the news saying they will not change their life. We wonder.

A small business owner or working partner who has just won the lottery might turn to his manager or partner and say, "Here are the office keys and a check for $50,000. I'll have my attorney contact you and I'll come by next week to answer any questions you have. Then again, the lawyer will call, but I'll probably not be coming back. Good luck and good-bye." If a key employee or your partner wins, you could be left ill-equipped, holding those keys, the proverbial "bag," and wondering what to do.

4. EXHAUSTION

Exhaustion happens when business or life's struggles have worn the owner down, and he hasn't or won't give up. He's a fighter and refuses to let go. The six and seven-day work weeks, the 10 to 14-hour days have drained the life spirit from him. While he may be present at work, he's cynical, depressed and resigned. If his spouse and children haven't left, they might as well have. Joy and possibility are memories. Customers are tolerated with and it shows.

Now the opposite can also be true. Equally important, the venture's ongoing success could represent a very real risk to *your* continued well-being. If the success relies solely on you, the all-consuming responsibility can lead to stress-related physical and emotional illness.

Mitigate The Risks!

These are just a few of the risks you and your organization face. This complex interdependence applies to you and other important leaders in your business as well.

Everything I'm saying here applies regardless of whether the enterprise is large or small, for-profit or non-profit. Later we'll address more unique aspects, but at this point, succession and exit affect all organizations from the Fortune 100 to PTA committees and your business unit.

If you successfully pass on your venture, you likely will have a strong vested interest in the continued viability of your business. Let's say, five years from now you're no longer closely associated with the business but are depending upon a stream of payments from it. Perhaps your successor does poorly and cannot maintain the payments to you and you are unable to step back in. The business crashes and your lifeline payments stop. Read on; learn how to lessen this possibility.

Three Strikes Can Take You Out

You have probably encountered some of these dilemmas in your firm or you've seen them occur in the businesses of colleagues. Sometimes there are multiple complications. A family member is diagnosed with a serious illness. A year or two later an accident involves a key employee. The owner is overwhelmed and exhausted.

Many businesses close their doors within days or weeks of a calamity. Family members retain one or more employees part-time to re-organize, run a "going-out-of-business" sale, sell inventory, equipment and client lists to an industry colleague or competitor. They salvage what they can. The proceeds from such closures are a fraction of the value of the business when it was open and vibrant the week before.

IRS tax code is structured so business buyers have tax advantages if they purchase assets. Business sellers typically have tax advantages when selling corporation stock, and fewer advantages when selling assets. This sets up the dynamic that when a seller *must* sell, the buyer frequently can dictate the terms for buying assets only. When there is no choice, those assets may go for 5 to 20 cents on the dollar.

Many assets considered intangibles, like a client list, the company phone number, and trade secrets, *can* be packaged, marketed and sold. This can be done if, and only if, the folks preparing the business for sale have the time and expertise and are able to package and sell those intangibles. Otherwise, this value is lost.

What happens if you are suddenly disabled or you die? What kinds of decisions are your heirs going to be forced to make because you did not prepare? Is your business structured so staff can operate it with or without you? If not, systematizing your business should be your next step toward the main goal of preparing to transfer ownership.

It's obvious that a business owner should stay physically fit and healthy, build cash reserves, diversify investments, hold no debt and maintain great insurance. But no matter how well organized a business is, when an owner is incapacitated or dies, the venture may well face a dramatic risk of closure. Your goal should be to reduce that risk as much as possible.

Demonstrating Leadership

When a firm has a leader who is a genius and crucial to operations there can be significant opportunities, but also great risk. The more dependent the company is upon the genius leader, the greater the urgency to craft and maintain a management system with a succession and exit plan for that leader.

Any disruption in the abilities of the owner or an interruption in routine services could result in permanent customer and revenue loss. In consulting circles, I've heard this kind of client referred to as a 9-1-1 case.

Regardless of the size or situation of your business, you, as the owner, have chosen the role of leadership. Use the rational skills of strategy, opportunity and threat to consider your alternatives and craft a prudent course for your business future. This is what differentiates you, as owner, from being an employee in someone else's venture. Your paramount responsibility, as owner, is to lead, even if you are just leading yourself!

As you read, your rational mind is deliberating about how these opportunities and risks compare to your current life and business circumstance. Are we over-thinking these mortality and disability risks? What is your gut reaction?

Our objective is to create a business structure that trains regular, entry-level employees to grow in skill, and to make sound decisions and to work in teams to support each other and complete larger projects.

Owners sometimes dream of hiring a genius or industry savant to "solve" their problems. Or the owner is such a genius. Both cases are risky because the rest of the staff comes to depend on upon that person instead of taking individual responsibility and acting. The "genius" must be in the *system*, not any individual. Individuals come and go. When each employee contributes to making the system more intelligent, that business is more sustainable.

An organization dependent upon one or a few genius-like individuals is at risk of loss of one or all of their experts or of being held for ransom by the high value, and probably, high-priced expert. Build an expert *system* which anyone with average ability can learn from, operate and produce remarkable services and products. This is a more viable arrangement than one with a few employees with unusual gifts. The more gifted the owner, the more difficult it may be for him or her to make a successful exit unless the owner's gift is mentoring and inspiring the team.

We'll discuss ways a venture can take steps towards a better organization and smart systems in the coming pages. It begins with strategy.

Ask yourself,

- *What is my objective?*

- *What's most important?*

- *What are my priorities?*

- *What are the steps to reach upcoming milestones?*

2

CHAPTER 2 - BUSINESS VALUATION

———————

Most small business owners either grossly overvalue or undervalue their ventures.

Three components of business value are:

1. Assets for multiple uses beyond just your business,
2. Potential growth in cash flow and net profit supported by tax returns,
3. Your operations, represented by dependable staff using efficient systems to satisfy established clientele.

Purchasers of small businesses want information about net cash flow and net income. Net cash flow is money in, minus money out equals money remaining. Net income is sales less costs and expenses. Both use "money in" representing sales cash deposited to a bank during a period of time, such as a month. "Money out" is represented by costs of goods sold and expenses such as overhead paid from the bank or credit cards. Both net cash flow and net income are funds available for payment of debt and use by management for stockholder payment. Both net cash flow and net income represent cash basis, rather than accrual basis accounting.

(NOTE TO READER – These are crucial concepts for business shoppers and any business owner or stockholder. The leader of any organization simply must understand and work daily with these principles. If you don't understand this clearly, ask your accountant to explain it.)

What Is The Value Of Your Business?

Buyers want to know a firm's genuine net profit as supported by tax returns. Few serious buyers give much credence to a seller who says their federal returns are purposefully low to avoid taxes. It may be true, but in that case, the buyer has a very strong negotiating position to drive a valuation and offered price downward.

Another way to look at value is to consider the customers, staff and functioning equipment as all contributing to value. In an efficient operation, these components result in revenue and cash flow, net profit, assets, and equity. Repeat customers, efficient staff, modern equipment can each potentially increase the value of the business. However, all components must work together to comprise a functioning unit.

Practice Shopping For A Business

A good exercise for a business owner is to research and practice how to buy a business. I recommend proceeding as if you were buying investment real estate. Answer these questions:

- *What is for sale?*

- *What is the purchase price?*

- *What is the monthly probable cash flow and profit?*

- *What are the obligations and risk?*

- *What are the improvement costs?*

- *What is the probable resale price?*

With these facts and estimates, you will know the estimated monthly and final return on investment to evaluate the risk.

When operating a business, I recommend a similar approach. What have you invested and what do you plan to invest? What is your monthly and final expected return on investment?

Satisfying established clientele with your dependable staff, and using efficient systems and assets are key drivers in the value of any operation. Even with few employees, your business still has value, which you can bolster and transfer.

I speak with entrepreneurs with one or just a few employees who declare they have nothing to sell. The business name is their own personal name, they have a computer and some fixtures or equipment long depreciated. They tell me flatly, there is *nothing* here to sell! Typically, there is a combination of certainty and resignation in their voice.

The following are examples of transferable value that you may not have considered.

- The business phone number
- A valuable lease in a desirable location
- Loyal, competent employees
- A growing customer base and updated database of customer contact info
- Facebook and other social media
- An app created for customers
- The business name and brand
- An established delivery service system
- A current, inviting business website and effective Internet presence

The list can go on and on. All of these elements have value. It may take creativity to find a way to capture and sell that value, but that doesn't mean it cannot be done.

Determining A Business Value

Determining the value of a business is more complex than for a house or car. For houses and cars, there are comparative sales and valuation services readily available. Zillow.com and Kelley Blue Book are examples of services for determining home and auto values.

Quantifying the value of your business involves several interrelated activities. Assets and liabilities are studied in greater detail than just the balance sheet. Historical and recent financial trends are compared. Expected relationships with customers, vendors and competitors are studied. Marketing strategy, merchandising plans, budgets, risk and projected cash flow are mapped to create a range of possible values for your business.

The same business can have a different value depending on the buyer.

TYPES OF BUYERS

- Competitors – may buy your firm to absorb assets and reduce competition.

- Vendors – may buy your firm to enjoy the retail profit as well as their wholesale profit.

- Employees – have watched you and think they can do better or at least as well.

- Family Members – have been taught by you, want to carry on the family tradition and believe they can do it.

- Financial Investors – value your cash flow, net profit and possibly undervalued assets.

I propose that just the process of determining the value of a business in and of itself actually *increases* the value. That's right, with each element of the value process completed, the value itself will be increased. The reason is that for most small businesses these processes are vague, incomplete or non-existent. Not having these elements spelled out increases risk and therefore reduces value.

> ## Persuaded He Had Something to Sell
>
> I met Adam at a professional association. He was a single consultant who worked internationally. He'd developed deep technical skills and was in demand in firms in many countries. He told me one morning that he was going to stop working and retire soon. I questioned him why would he just "stop," and not *sell* his business. He said that he had no real business to sell, it was just him. "What can I sell? I have a couple computers, a desk, bookcases and technical books. There is nothing to sell!"
>
> I reminded him of the hundreds of clients who have called his phone number, written emails to him and gone to his website to get answers to their problems. Many of these folks would continue to call, email and look for him for some time after he might discontinue services, even if he tries to tell them he's retired. I reminded him of his customer list and the trusted relationships he'd built, his reputation in his industry. Surely there is someone, some competitor he's worked with and respects that would benefit by his sharing the good will he'd established – for a price.
>
> At subsequent meetings, he told me how he'd identified a section of his business, organized and sold that segment to a competitor for $60,000. He has continued in other parts of his work which are less demanding and he continues in business today.

Step-By-Step Valuation

The following is an overview of how to determine a simple business value.

DESCRIBE YOUR BUSINESS

Major customers, vendors and competitors, as well as the firm's place in the market should be described and analyzed objectively. Write about your firm's history: How did the firm begin? Who began it and why? What has occurred since the business started? Then write a few sentences or a couple paragraphs about what's going on for the company recently. You decide the time frame of days, weeks or months. If you were writing to an old business friend, what would you say to explain the firm's current circumstance and how it got there.

LIST YOUR ASSETS

Make a list of assets. Include both physical and intangible assets. A physical asset list can be made in a spreadsheet with columns for the price paid, date bought, depreciation to date, the year you expect to replace the asset, replacement cost and your estimate of its liquidation value if you were to sell it.

LIST YOUR OBLIGATIONS

In a list of obligations include all debt, the balance due, description of the item purchased that created the debt, monthly payments and interest rate and term remaining on the debt. Other obligations are leases and all contracts for products, such as copiers or cell phones. Other ongoing obligations could include insurance, employee benefits for retirement, bonuses or promised salary increases.

Another obligation list could be regular recurring expenses such as payroll, utilities, and rent.

As you can see, this is a more detailed financial picture than a typical balance sheet or financial statement. A well-done asset and obligations summary with an accurate balance sheet begins to better describe the main components in an organization's valuation.

CHART REVENUES

The next step in determining the value of your business is a description of revenue, costs of goods, and net profit annually and perhaps seasonally for the last three to five years with comparisons between last year and the current year-to-date. Compare and analyze monthly and quarterly totals.

NOW SWOT IT!

SWOT is an acronym for strengths, weaknesses, opportunities, threats. A SWOT is a structured planning method begun in the 1960s to evaluate the internal and external, positive and negative aspects involved in achieving a specific objective. A SWOT can be used for a company, product, place, industry or person. Your firm's current circumstances can be described with a SWOT: Strengths, Weaknesses, Opportunities and Threats (SWOT). Build upon the above-mentioned description of relationships with major clients, vendors and competitors and the industry as it affects your business. Close this with a long-term outlook for the next two to ten years.

OUTLINE YOUR PLAN

From these descriptions, individual reports can be prepared to outline your plans to expand clientele and the changes you want to make to your mix of products and services to better fulfill your clients' changing needs. Add a review of the strengths and weaknesses of your vendor alliances and options you have if a major vendor fails to perform.

CONDUCT A COMPETITIVE ANALYSIS

Prepare a competitive analysis of the other industry players serving your clients. What firms are filling the needs of clients like yours in adjacent markets who might decide to enter your market? How does your marketing and merchandising strategy compare?

WORK THE NUMBERS

Substantiate your views with simple overview financial scenarios. Build scenario spreadsheets for probable, best and worst case financial projections. The next 12 months should be done by month based upon those same months in prior years. A simple cash flow projection showing estimated revenue, cost of goods sold, staff payroll, officers' compensation, and all other expenses, including debt service, can be built by month for at least 12 months and preferably 24 months. Once done it's easy to extend the cash projection by quarters for two to five years to substantiate your strategic product development, marketing, merchandising and competitive plans.

GOOD WILL

Good will is the respect and admiration the public has in a company. Good will is a complex subject and of great importance in business operations and valuation. Google defines good will as a noun and the second meaning applies in business:

1. friendly, helpful, or cooperative feelings or attitude.

"the plan is dependent on good will between the two sides"

2. the established reputation of a business regarded as a quantifiable asset, e.g., as represented by the excess of the price paid at a takeover of a company over its fair market value.

Investopedia.com defines "good will" as an intangible asset that arises as a result of the acquisition of one company by another for a premium value. The value of a company's brand name, solid customer base, good customer relations, good employee relations and any patents or proprietary technology represent *good will*.

SELLING ASSETS

An asset is anything of value. A business owns assets, therefore a business is an asset. It can take time and money to transfer an asset properly. Using the principle of materiality, it's unwise to spend more on an asset than it is worth, whether that is to purchase it, transfer it or in many cases improve it. Sometimes, the value of an asset has dwindled so much it's sold at auction, donated to a non-profit or given away.

There may be many reasons why not to "sell" a business, and sell or transfer assets instead.

Here are two of many possible reasons to consider selling assets rather than the business entity. The company has operated at a loss, and assets and good will are worth less than the expense of improvement or transfer. Other reasons for not selling can include the transfer of the business or remaining assets to a family member or close friend. Some written agreement should always be prepared to explicitly outline what is being transferred and how. Learn how to write simple agreements, such as a legal receipt or a bill of sale. Without this knowledge, "informal transfers" can be dangerous and should be avoided. For tax and legal reasons, always get professional advice when transferring assets. All asset transfers should be recognized on federal tax returns. Failure to do so can have severe consequences which can be avoided by merely following the rules and getting professional assistance.

THE PROCESS OF VALUING

The process of valuing and then realizing the value you have determined may not be a process in which you are interested or competent to complete. Annual valuation by a professional can be done to be sure the firm is being managed in a responsible and sustainable fashion.

As mentioned above, under some circumstances the transfer or sale of assets is preferable to the sale of stock. There are risks when transferring a business. Sometimes buyers sue the seller when they feel they paid more than the business was worth. The business may be in a declining industry so the owner doesn't think there is much value to be transferred. Perhaps the cost of updating the firm is too costly or the effort too great for an owner to wish to work through the effort, expense and risk of polishing a "rotten apple" and then trying to sell it. Sometimes it makes sense to simply liquidate and close your doors.

Markets go up and down. Adverse market circumstances may dictate working on the business to sell (or not) at some future date. You may not know the date the market will rebound, but that's no reason not to begin preparation by improving the value of the business in every way you know how. As mentioned throughout this guide, improved management makes the venture easier to operate and potentially more profitable now. However, I advise you to improve the business value and be ready to sell quickly and smoothly when the market rebounds.

Some small businesses succeed when they are in a narrow niche market and the operator has multiple skills. The owner can do almost all the operational work themselves thus keeping expenses low and the venture profitable. The narrow niche market limits competition and the varied expertise of the owner allows the venture to shine among the few competitors it does have.

These market strengths that allow it to exist, however, limit the transferability of the venture. Only another leader with remarkable skills that is highly adaptable can replace this owner. It could be transferred to a competitor or to an industry expert. Someone with deep subject matter knowledge could be a candidate if they are committed to learning the skills necessary for business survival such as sales, order fulfillment, and bookkeeping.

Having dependable staff, even if the business is dependent upon you, can usually increase the business value. A profitable history and the anticipation of future profits are of great importance in the value of such an organization. With that caveat, it's recognized that a *systematized* business, one which will operate regardless of owner involvement, can be worth from one to ten times the value of a venture that is not.

A small business with one or a few dependable, experienced

employees may be purchased for a comparatively low price and turned into a systematized business by a knowledgeable buyer who is an effective manager. The buyer can organize, systematize and train a manager to replace himself thereby transforming a dependent business into one which the staff and manager can operate themselves. There is a much larger market for a structured venture operated by staff than one that requires an owner with expertise in that industry. Inversely, businesses which are less structured and more dependent upon owner involvement require a special buyer, thus reducing the field of potential purchasers. The new owner may need years of experience and advanced skills equal to or more expert than the current owner. This expansion or limitation of the field of buyers can significantly influence the value of a venture.

Ready to Sell Farm... If Prices and Demand Rise

Daniel was a contractor who moved onto 20+ acres in the rural northwest in 1983. He signed a contract to buy the land the following year. Over the years, he built a home and organic farm with an orchard, fish pond, goats, chickens, turkeys, and llamas. It's been his commercial construction work that's made it all possible. The farm requires an enormous amount of work to maintain.

Daniel has a large cold storage room where they keep the food they preserve and produce for sale to local natural food stores and markets. They would like to begin selling to restaurants.

For years Daniel had an accountant and tax preparer and each year he'd pay some taxes for his construction work. Eight years ago, his accountant died. In that year, his construction work increased so he hired a full-time employee beyond the occasional part time help he'd used. Then he got an IRS letter saying he owed $5,000. The national economy tanked shortly after and he fell behind on his mortgage. Now eight years have passed and he's still paying monthly on the $5,000 plus penalties and interest. He's probably paid the initial $5,000 tax claim and is now paying just interest and penalties.

Last year they began a long-planned bed and breakfast for folks wishing to visit an organic farm in the Oregon woods. They're attracting visitors nationally and internationally. He's gotten a new mortgage and is beginning to think of retiring from construction work. Farming work also is becoming too difficult for him to continue. He's focusing on increasing the business value beyond the real estate value so when he sells he can realize a return on his 35 years of hard, physical work.

During the economic challenge when he struggled and almost lost his farm in foreclosure, he again fell behind with accounting. Around 2011, I assisted Daniel in getting accounting reports to a new tax preparer so four years of returns could be filed. In the next year, we got two years accounting to a new preparer and his accounting current. With accurate accounting and tax returns he was able to sell the bed and breakfast farm and move on to his next career projects.

Lesson: It can and often does take years of accounting and tax returns to increase the business value beyond the value of the real estate.

3

CHAPTER 3 - STRATEGY AND ENTREPRENEURSHIP

To be an entrepreneur is to see an opportunity and a way to seize it. In its simplest form, that is Strategy.

A key question: Are there opportunities for 'economies of scale,' reductions in overhead or risk? Is this an opportunity for synchronicity where 1+1=3? Genuine leadership is needed to discern and capture fleeting opportunities. The ability to be strategic can be of great importance for your clients, yourself and your family.

Strategy – a word derived from French, Latin and Ancient Greek:

1. The science and art of military command as applied to the overall planning and conduct of warfare.

2. A plan of action intended to accomplish a specific goal.

3. The art of using similar techniques in politics or business.

Tactics – an English word

1. (military) The military science that deals with achieving the objectives set by strategy.

2. (military) Maneuvers used against an enemy.

3. (military) The employment and ordered arrangement of forces in relation to each other[1].

Strategy is determining what to do and why. "Tactics" are *how* to accomplish the strategy. These terms are relative to each other and can be used in layers. A broad strategy to reach a five-year objective has tactics for annual marketing. There can then be an annual advertising strategy with its own tactics. Both strategy and tactics are important in operating the business and preparing for a Smart Exit™.

Maintaining a Balanced Perspective

Real leaders assure that both the clients' needs and the organization's mission statement are realized now *and* tomorrow. Professional managers attempt to ensure that good days will continue next month and for years.

The responsibility of leadership is for the future as well as the present. Time and resources must be set aside for future leadership needs. Advanced training must be provided with new opportunities for staff to excel, to keep them interested and prevent their leaving at the first opportunity for advancement elsewhere.

Staff development and advancement opportunities are important because your firm needs more than just a next leader to replace you. The culture must be healthy and strong for your new leader to have a staff to inspire. The new leader can't do it alone. You didn't do it alone and our society is changing, requiring more complex organizations if they are to survive competitively.

Maturity is a key ingredient for business success. In this context, I use maturity as the ability to consider a variety of disparate important issues and to understand their interdependence. The crucial must be sorted from the worthwhile. Effective action must be taken, all while maintaining a balanced, positive perspective.

You must go beyond supervising the serving of clients, the marketing to new prospects, accounting, tax reports and computer maintenance. After all these valuable and important duties, time must be scheduled for advanced staff training for all who qualify and for special training to groom a new leader.

The firm must be generating enough revenue to pay a future leader enough to keep his or her interest and give him or her the necessary supervisory instruction and support. If you, yourself, can't provide all the advanced training the new leader will need, you have to find it, check it out, and then pay for the employee to receive it.

This all must be done in a way that the prospective leader, during training, doesn't get seduced and hired by your competitor, requiring you to start again with a new candidate. Staying in business has been difficult; transferring ownership and exiting smart can be *more* difficult.

DIFFERENT PERSPECTIVES

Being open to new ideas means being flexible, adaptive and creative. Blogs, videos, lectures and reading business books contribute to one's understanding of the enormous cultural changes our society is experiencing. We must empathize with and appreciate how these technological and economic shifts influence the values and beliefs of our customers, employees, and community. Look forward, into your business future.

There are new business models and tools being developed by thought leaders and in university entrepreneurship centers. They distinguish small and medium enterprises (SME) from "innovation-driven" enterprises (IDE).

IDEs are fast growth firms appealing to Internet and global customers which focus on universal needs beyond the peculiarities of local markets. Small and medium businesses (SME) grow to a certain size and then stop. Most organizations, (probably your firm) are small to medium businesses.

SMEs are learning how to become innovation driven. Innovation driven business models are being found useful, not only for fast growth new venture launches but also for existing and mature firms to revamp tired management methods with new product and market initiatives. In many markets, SMEs must become innovation driven to compete and survive.

Staying abreast of new business practices can be daunting. Below is a sampling of new business models and tools to taste, sample and see what you might like to consider testing in your organization.

Audio books, podcasts, YouTube, web searches and tips from colleagues lead to new ideas. Here are the ideas of a few thought leaders I've come to value. Explore Smart-Exit.com and BeCauseBusiness.com for continuing management ideas, business tools, models, and suggestions. Join the Be Cause Membership Community to exchange ideas and suggest your favorite models, tools, authors, and speakers.

"Disciplined Entrepreneurship"
Bill Aulet outlines 24 steps to a successful startup in his book "Disciplined Entrepreneurship."[1] Aulet believes: 1) entrepreneurship can be taught and 2) being a charismatic leader isn't required. There's a series of steps to a successful launch of an innovative product.

With this focused, integrated framework, a person willing to invest the effort can build their current venture or launch a new effort. Aulet is managing director of the Martin Trust Center for MIT Entrepreneurship and a senior lecturer at the MIT Sloan School of Management.

"Lean Startup"
"...an organization dedicated to creating something new under conditions of extreme uncertainty" is Eric Reis' definition of a startup. New or mature, I say this is the challenge every business leader is facing today. Reis builds a case for testing very simple

---

1. Bill Aulet. *Disciplined Entrepreneurship.* Hoboken NJ: John Wiley & Sons, 2013.

business models to create "validated learning." Features can be added once the basic model is proven.

Reis calls this the "minimum viable product." He advocates testing the vision continuously, adapting and adjusting to make it right from the earliest experiments. Why not use a scientific model to innovate, learn, apply, test, and apply? Relentless development is the mantra in his book "Lean Startup: How Today's Entrepreneurs Use Continuous Innovation to Create Radically Successful Businesses.[2]"

"Business Model Generation"

If you're struggling to create new or re-create your existing business models and design for tomorrow's marketplace, there are tools to create new "what-if" strategies. Alexander Osterwalder and Yves Pigneur have co-created strategic ideas which are easy to implement with the help of 470 "business model canvas" practitioners from 45 countries. They have produced two books that work independently or together. *Business Model Generation* is the overview and *Value Proposition Design*[3] focuses on the model's core dynamics.

"The Living Organization"

A business is more than a machine with its sales, products, purchases, and numbers. Corporations are by definition separate legal entities from the owner(s). There is "corporate personhood" and beyond that, your organization is a living being. What kind of being is your organization? Is it male or female, an infant or

---

2. Reis, Eric. *Lean Startup: How Today's Entrepreneurs Use Continuous Innovation to Create Radically Successful Businesses.* New York, NY: Crown Business Random House, Inc., 2011.
3. Alexander Osterwalder *et al., Business Model Generation* and *Value Proposition Design.* Hoboken NJ: John Wiley & Sons, 2011 and 2014.

mature? What kind of relationships does it have, internally and externally? Go beyond your vision, mission, value statements. What is your organization's Soulful Purpose? Why are you here?

What's your Living Organization's Strategic Compass that will guide and align all living parts of the organization? Author Norman Wolfe dives deeper into the core elements of "process, people, customer, finance," revealing how the energy of "activity, relationship, context" impacts each of these business dimensions. Wolfe addresses how to maximize the flow of all the energy of an organization to create extraordinary impact. Make magic happen for customers and staff – *The Living Organization: Transforming Business To Create Extraordinary Results.*"[4]

Professional Assistance

Review these ideas with your accountant, attorney, and banker and they will support the argument I am advancing.

We're giving you a cluster of pertinent organizational concepts in summary form, a working introduction. Reading this guide is a good start, but not enough. Reading will help, but only as you can diligently implement the concepts and reshape your organization can these methods take root and assist you in identifying staff with potential. Then you must train, mentor and groom staff with particular attention to one or two key leaders to whom you may possibly transfer responsibility.

There are many qualified management consultants and business coaches with skills and resources similar to those that Be Cause

4. Wolfe, Norman. *The Living Organization: Transforming business To Create Extraordinary Results.* Irvine CA: Quantum Leaders Publishing, 2011.

Business uses to train clients. Through the Institute of Management Consultants, we collaborate with many of them.

Crafting the legal agreements whereby the new leader can successfully take over the business is another hurdle. Establishing a win-win agreement with security and tax-advantaged retirement planning for you will be an advanced step in your journey.

The agreement must allow the new leader to demonstrate they can:

- Learn from you
- Innovate with your help and later on their own
- Advance the firm with a dynamic staff, so all of you can become more successful

The company must be able to pay the new leader a viable income and also pay you for your years of hard work.

A succession and exit team typically includes:

- Accountant
- Attorney
- Insurance broker
- Investment broker
- Valuation expert
- Business exit consultant

A specially trained business exit consultant guides the team while you are preparing for growth so the firm has the finances to attract and secure a viable candidate. Then the consultant and your team support you as you work with the candidate.

This sounds hard. Of course it is hard. This hand-off from teacher to student, expert to novice, father to son, mother to daughter, employer to employee has gone on for thousands of years. Trade apprenticeship programs are built upon these methods. It is hard. But it can and is being done. With support, you can do it, and with help, you may do it well.

Your attitude is ultimately your biggest asset or liability. As entrepreneurs, we fail when we give up.

"Whether you think that you can, or that you can't, you are usually right." – Henry Ford.

There is hope! We can always do better if we begin today. The past is gone. What can we do today to improve tomorrow? Smart Exit™? You bet. Let's do it!

4

CHAPTER 4 - REASONING AND INNOVATION

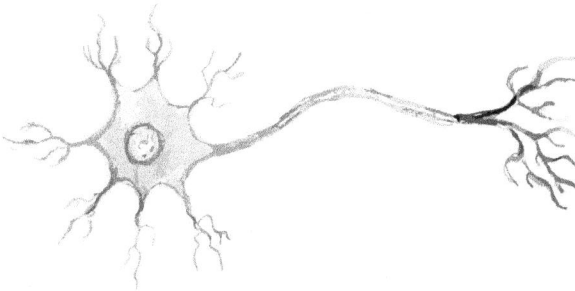

Can You Imagine?

Our neurons bring our world into being. Do you understand how you can grow and tend to them in ways to reach your business objectives and life goals?

I hope you are very comfortable using your imagination to figure out solutions. When facing a dilemma, abstract thinking and your imagination are your best allies. Your cognitive abilities have been a critical asset in first launching and then administering your business all these years.

You've used your creative imagination throughout your career. You are gifted in seeing what's possible for your firm. You market to attract new, significant clients. You navigate and master cash flow, build reserves and pay down debt.

Determine What Obstacle To Solve Next

Limitations in your reasoning, innovation and imagination may be the obstacle to concluding this chapter of your career and moving on to the next. Your ability to envision what is *now* possible for your firm is your big, immediate challenge. Coupled with seeing your firm's future is imagining the possible future for your firm's next leader and you.

By imagining the future for your firm, the next leader and yourself, you will better understand possible opportunities and engage your team in seizing them. To change the life you've been leading to what your life can now become, map the steps to each objective.

The daily grind can reduce our ability to think deeply. Mindless repetition, overloading our conscious awareness with massive detail or endless meetings, all deplete our mental reserves. In the latest studies, new, challenging complex thinking is the best way to maintain and even increase cognitive abilities at any age, according to Dr. Sandra Bond Chapman, founder and director of the Brain Health Center at the University of Texas.[1]

Identifying your most likely successor from among your seasoned employees or family, then preparing them to become the owner will require giving that person significant advanced training. That advanced training will take time. But unlike your experience starting and administering your own business for years, the grooming of a new leader involves special skill and risk.

Don't Train A New Competitor

If done wrong, you could be training a competitor who will leave with your trade secrets to compete against you. You will need a legally-binding, written agreement for protection early in the process. A good way to begin is with employment agreements for all your staff. As soon as the aspiring leader shows genuine interest, aptitude and partner potential, it's time for an agreement in principle that can reduce the risk of creating a turncoat who could become your most powerful competitor.

You could spend a couple years training someone before that candidate fails and you must find a new candidate. If you have a medical emergency, the new candidate may not be fully ready

---

1. Chapman, Dr. Sandra Bond. *Make Your Brain Smarter: An Easy Plan to Increase Your Creativity, Energy, and Focus*. New York, NY: Simon & Schuster Inc., 2013.

to take over. But having a trusted employee with some advanced management training would certainly be better than no such employee.

Organization leaders must routinely model learning and practice self-improvement skills for themselves, their staff and leader candidates. Mental exercises are being researched and developed by brain scientists to overcome the restrictions that have limited our abilities.

Genuine leaders study and perfect their own improvement, building the abilities of employees who can do tasks with skill greater than the leader himself. It's been said the best teachers help their student to progress beyond them. So too, the leader preparing his successor must nurture the new leader to develop staff so they can actualize more of their personal potential to help the organization and themselves.

Aging and Health

There is a revolution occurring in brain research that is validating the thought that humans can maintain cognitive abilities, growing new neurons and connections until death, according to Dr. Norman Doidge in *The Brain That Changes Itself.*[2] Challenging mental activities and robust physical fitness can continue to engender strategic reasoning and innovation until our final days so long as we exert the effort to continue learning.

"Brain fitness" needs to be included in any physical fitness regime. You don't want your body to outlive your brain. Longer lives and

---

2. Doidge, Dr. Norman. *The Brain That Changes Itself: Stories of Personal Triumph From the Frontier of Brain Science.* New York, NY: Penguin Group Inc., 2007.

the surge of aging baby boomers are combining to amplify the dementia problem. A cure for dementia and Alzheimer's is being sought but has not yet been found. Nor has a way been found to prevent them. But robust brain and physical health have been found to forestall dementia and Alzheimer's while adding years of quality life after early diagnosis. Maintaining your brain health should be a priority. And anything that supports and amplifies the brain health of an organization's leader and its staff members supports and amplifies the organization's "brain."

Administrative Skills

Being able to scale a business up with a combination of incremental improvements and occasional transformational leaps when opportunities arise requires different skills and temperament than an entrepreneurial start-up specialist.

In "Smart Exit™," I am offering an instruction and prediction practice to guide you, the owner, to optimize your organization in several key ways. Improve your operations and staff involvement while increasing sales and profit. Revenue (your sales and marketing department) and systems (your order fulfillment team) must be improved in tandem to have a lasting benefit (net profit).

As you develop staff, you will identify a potential leader whom you can mentor as the employees watch you grow the venture. This new leader may come from inside or you may attract someone from outside. You can teach them by showing them. As they learn, they will assist and accelerate your progress. Can you imagine seeing yourself applying new methods for operating, instructing, managing and inspiring your staff, your firm's new leader and the stakeholders who will propel your venture forward?

Do this and the value of the business will grow; so, too, will the asking price you can command. Your venture will appeal to a larger group of potential buyers and it will be easier to operate while you own it and faster to transfer when you decide to step out. I call this a Smart Exit™ strategy!

Visualize this: See yourself beginning your next project as you step away from your current firm. See both activities being adroitly managed. See yourself finding greater peace and happiness than you have ever known. Visualizing activity as a mental practice has been found to be virtually as effective as actual performance. Visualize your firm moving forward without you. Let's take the next steps to actualize the possibility we are creating together.

Reach Toward World Class

Reach toward being a *world-class* organization beginning today! It starts with you, here and now, deciding to apply the professional management tools you have known would be good to do but which you may have struggled to find the time and resources to actually do.

A reliable way to exit is to build new tools into your firm's culture, and then train and mentor staff to use them. Then, use critical measurements of your firm, sometimes called Key Performance Indicators or KPI, to observe the company as you pull away. Develop the KPI with staff for them to use and for you to assist them in using. This Smart Exit™ guide is your first step. Smart Exit™ will point you in the right direction. It starts with you today. We are available to answer questions and assist with hurdles where you might stumble. We'll throw you a line if we see your sails ragged and your rudder broken.

As you successfully apply tools such as KPI, budgets, strategy and project management, your staff morale and quality of goods to customers will improve. Revenue and profit will follow.

Upon conclusion of this nautical adventure, you'll have an opportunity to take these skills and apply them in your ongoing strategy, project management, and staff development. Your venture will only be as successful as your staff can adapt to future customer needs, leading, not following, your competitors. Let's have some fun and see what we can imagine and create!

You've been the leader of your organization for years. What new projects *beyond* the firm are awaiting you? Got a new idea, a new firm or travel, family, and fun? Are you ramping up for a new challenge or is your biggest challenge reshaping what you've built so you can move on?

By reading, *and implementing* this book you will grow the value of your business, identify and mentor a successor, sell the business to the new leader and make your Smart Exit™!

Hire A Coach

Do you have a master coach to guide you and later your successor? Don't need one? Are you doing your own tax returns? Have you tried defending yourself in a court of law?

Perspective and objectivity when facing important decisions are crucial. Staying on track, concluding with the funds actually in the retirement account and no lawsuits are what you want. Sometimes when you need help, you should ask for the best that your money can buy. This may be the only time you have prepared to transfer a business you've owned for many years. Can you risk a failure? How many times are you prepared to "practice" before you get it right?

The coach who helps you transfer to your successor plays a valuable role "bridging" your involvement. As the successor gains traction it will be the coach to whom he or she increasingly turns, allowing you greater freedom to come and go. Ongoing meetings between you, the successor and the coach allow you to monitor and influence the successor's future while the company gradually requires less and less of your direct involvement.

Hire a master coach from whom you can learn as well, and practice coaching your succession candidate. You know how to give direct orders. Learn to ask open-ended questions to give the candidate a safe space to think through answers and grow. Encourage, correct and support this person's management training.

The successor's written strategy, budgets, and targets will enable communications between the two of you, while improving his or her chances of continued growth and eventual success for all of you: the firm, the successor and you. The successor will be little more equipped than you to use these tools unless your company culture drives all your staff to work within these best practice methods together. The staff must work together, or they will be like the dated three-ring binders on the shelf, covered with dust and cobwebs, laughed at and dismissed.

Your Business As A Trading Galleon

There are a variety of specialized skills I want to share with you to increase your management tools. Part Two in Smart Exit™, Business Navigation, is a nautical adventure into operating your business as if it were a 16th-century sailing galleon trading from port to port. During this voyage, you'll experience the benefits of analyzing your venture. Once an analysis has been conducted, we'll consider your systems and methods.

We'll look at innovation in what you're doing, how it's done and why. You'll learn fundamentals in scaling organizations up *and* down so you can adjust to varying economic tides and storms. Then we'll consider communications. We will examine the internal and external cultures you've created and how you might adjust your message to better suit and anticipate your customers' changing needs and tastes.

You will review your current circumstances, history, finances and consider your future. After you read this book or some parts of it, you may offer it to your partner or a key manager. This book, combined with a class, could foster a mentoring program you develop for staff. It is with your inner team, your key employees and possibly a leader-in-training that you work collectively to test and implement these strategies.

MOST importantly, you can create a mentoring program that fits you and your leading candidate. Want to learn more about mentoring a new leader? Read on!

New strategies will be built from the successes and lessons learned from your past and what's leading your industry today. We will consider the hunches and inklings that might put you into market leadership rather than play catch-up. Over and over, we'll revisit the identification of a candidate, then their preparation as your successor.

Part II

Part II - Business Navigation

There are a variety of ways companies and non-profit organizations are transferred.

Two fundamental transfer methods involve attorneys writing legal agreements and accountants facilitating straightforward financial structures for exchange of assets. Attorneys specialize in many fields, of which business law is one. Attorneys are trained to craft legal agreements. Ownership transfer of businesses is a complex field requiring special training, education and years of experience to be fully competent.

Accountants who have earned Certified Public Accountant or Internal Revenue Service Enrolled Agent status are educated to structure financial transfers. But like attorneys, financial transfer of corporations and limited liability companies is a specialty field. Manufacturers, restaurants, and commercial contractors, for example, each represent specific accounting and valuation issues that require continuous experience in that industry to maintain expert knowledge. Each industry has specialty knowledge and history. The generalist attorney or accountant must research to be competent in different business fields. In addition, while the legal and financial vehicles are the bedrock of ownership transfers, they aren't everything.

Small, one or two-owner ventures are sometimes called "closely-held," meaning there are few partners, stockholders and company officers. These partners typically know each other, live in the same state and frequently are employees and company officers. Some find it surprising, but even proprietorships, simple partnerships, single owner and closely-held corporations can be very complex and have a value of many millions of dollars. Beyond obvious tangible assets, there are variety of business values which traditional legal and financial structures can struggle to articulate and describe.

Leadership directing intangible assets to leverage physical properties can be better distinguished by highly experienced CEOs, CFOs, executive managers and professional management consultants trained in transfer of formal authority. On the other hand, turn-around experts and bankruptcy trustees are skilled at stepping into highly dynamic business emergencies to restore order and capture values to transfer safely.

There are experts in management, finance, administration, marketing and operations who can prepare ventures to scale business up and down and merge or transfer. These leadership and management experts are frequently more capable of organizing intangible assets such as staffing, brand, culture, communication and marketing strategies to protect or enhance public opinion, market share/position for firms, products and services.

For firms with a recognized value of at least $1 million, those assisting in commercial transfer can include:

* Venture capitalists,

* Investors,

* Securities brokers,

* Merger and acquisition teams and

* Management consultants.

In general, these experts seek to increase the value of the organization in a variety of ways, then market the better organized entity for a substantially greater value. This allows the manager or team to recover their investment, time and risk.

Each of these categories uses traditional and highly creative methods to attract new investors. They bring to firms a wide variety of new assets including a new perspective, expertise, cash, short and long term debt and equity funding, markets, staff and industry contacts.

Experts may have established markets in the form of single large investors, investor groups, Initial Public Offerings (IPOs), penny stocks and makers of other special markets.

Employee Stock Option Plans (ESOPs) and cooperative ventures are other specialty ownership/management vehicles. While different in some ways from regular corporations, management control of non-profits can be transferred in similar ways, though they must be consistent with IRS rules and regulations.

Fees to transfer firms with a value of at least $1 million, can exceed 10% of company value. Merger & Acquisition fees would begin at $100,000 to $200,000. For firms with a value of less than $1 million, management consultants, business brokers and commercial real estate brokers have long functioned helping firms transfer along with attorneys and experienced accountants.

Each type of specialist has certain typical types of education, training, expertise, benefits and short comings. These specialists serve firms both the above and below $1 million value.

It's generally accepted that 50% or more of all business transfers have at least one significant flaw. But with the assistance of trusted experts, a successful transfer can be accomplished in the desirable time period and at a cost the seller is willing to pay.

CHAPTER 5 - AND A HARDY SHIP SHE IS!

———————

Steer your trading galleon to the rewards you deserve!

Craft your business to:

- *Gracefully fulfill the needs of customers*
- *Operate efficiently and profitably without your daily involvement, and*
- *Be transferable to new owners at almost any point in the event of an emergency or by your decision.*

Smart ships have dependable power and navigation tools to avoid the reefs that are littered with ships that strayed off course. For thousands of years, explorers on sailing vessels traded goods from port to port, rarely leaving sight of land. Dead reckoning navigation, early maps, and star charts enabled merchants to cross oceans. Risk has been gradually reduced with the compass and sextant, followed by radio, radar, satellites and global cell phones. Sail and wind power were replaced by steam, diesel, nuclear, natural gas, electric and solar.

Are you an "old salt" with years of experience?

Are you considering how you might promote a promising lieutenant to become the new captain?

Preparing for a leadership change can be a good time to upgrade tools and methods. Vessels can be refitted, updated and modernized to incorporate the technology and deep cultural changes hurtling us forward.

Your Business Adventure

Smart Exit™ is for both experienced and new leaders. It is a nautical adventure, an exploration aboard your sailing galleon into how you might optimize it for yourself and the leaders who will follow you. Prepare for the next leader *now* and you'll accelerate your ease of management and the accomplishments you achieve.

What is the level of technology you are depending upon? How up to date are your computer systems, operational competitiveness, and marketing prowess? Instinct, natural ability, talent, some fundamental business education and experience have brought you this far. But what is the risk to your vessel and crew? Do you deliver your cargo and fulfill promises to your clients, stakeholders, and family? Could you do better?

How many more years will you be captain and commander? You may not be on the next voyage of this ship. With any luck, you will soon identify that promising lieutenant, fully train him or her as a new captain, and he or she will be at the wheel. On this voyage, you are grooming the crew and looking for that new leader to prepare for the future.

These are challenging times. Are you risking years of your effort and the well-being of your family and your employees' families with a poorly trained crew using outdated business tools? Do you want your venture to sink, survive, or thrive?

Can your company and the new leader dependably pay you for your years of service as you step away? You may have a smartphone, but do you have a smart ship with a capable captain and crew?

Think Like a Venture Capitalist

I want to invite you, as a smart captain, to look carefully into the future of your business. Learn from serial entrepreneurs who have proven themselves successful by building businesses that they sell. With that revenue, they venture their capital into the firm(s) they help to build, prepare for transfer and then sell.

I'm talking about venture capitalists. I want to invite you to *consider yourself a venture capitalist* from this day forward. If you can, it will reshape how you look at your business. Be objective. Don't blindly spend a huge investment in hours and dollars to take big and un-calculated risks.

A venture capitalist invests money and frequently business expertise to make a good business idea a practical, working reality. Traditionally, venture capitalists bring money and expertise to an entrepreneur who has a business or is beginning a business but realizes he needs help beyond his means. I invite one part of you, the realist, to be the venture capitalist, to help another part of you, the entrepreneur with a dream.

Venture capitalists typically have a cardinal rule. When considering a business, they will not invest without 1) a specific, expected return on their investment, and 2) an exit date. They require a clearly written plan spelling out how they will proceed from entry to exit showing action steps, cash flow prediction and alternative scenarios for the expected tricky parts. They know these plans will change, but it is with these tools that they manage the venture to reduce risk and increase their success rate.

They compare the prudent possible gain from their investment against their risk of loss. They compare the gain and risk in a prospective venture to low gain and low-risk investments like bonds, annuities, secured notes or mutual funds. How does your business' gain-to-risk ratio compare to "safer" but lower gain choices?

If you can maintain this fundamental perspective it will give you greater objectivity in your business decisions. It will assist you to see clearly when you might otherwise feel confused and unsure. Remember, your business is not just a job where you show up and perform endless duties. You have a greater purpose and because of your initiative owning and operating a business, you can sell that business and get paid back for the effort you've put forth, the risk you've wagered and the successful venture you can transfer ownership of to a successor.

Set Your Dollar & Date

Today, decide a date in the future when you might realistically transfer your business. Then work toward increasing the value of the business as you proceed toward that date. Be prepared to revise the date earlier or later as your needs, desires and circumstances dictate.

We all have networks of support to *be* in this world, to create, give and receive. The ideas I am sharing are familiar to you. You understand and fundamentally believe in many of these concepts.

These are simple, rational ideas: Prepare, think ahead and reduce risk. In the event of premature disability or death, we all wish to spare our families suffering and confusion. If and when you must stop what you've done for years and someone else must step in and make sense of your business and financial life, I'm sure you want that process to be as graceful as possible.

Like life insurance, estate and retirement planning, burial or cremation plans, this work can be confronting. When you chose to become an entrepreneur, you implicitly agreed to be responsible in a larger sense. You spoke up and declared, like the Jewish founder of a dynasty of sages, Hillel the Elder who said in the first century BC, *"If not you, then who; if not now, when?"* Of course, this isn't easy. Who said it would be? As the venture capitalist in you, what is your goal? Why are you investing your life blood into this business? Put it in writing and commit yourself. Tomorrow, you can change it, if necessary.

Take Action, NOW!

All organizations start as an idea. That idea, sometimes called an entrepreneur's insight, can be built into a functioning business to fulfill the needs of customers and in so doing, provide income for the staff and owners.

This Business Navigation program is an overview of established business practices which can be used as the fine tools of a master craftsman, a *business* craftsman. If you want to increase the value of your enterprise *AND* identify a capable successor with a reasonable chance of success, use these tools.

These tools can be used individually or in combination. How skillfully and how diligently you use them can influence how successful you are in building your venture.

> **Business Navigation Exercise**
>
> On what date will you exit your business and what will be your age?
>
> What amount of money would you like, or must you have when you exit?

6

CHAPTER 6 - ANALYSIS PRECEDES INNOVATION

"If the only tool you have is a hammer, you tend to see every problem as a nail."
Abraham Maslow

In the Introduction, we outlined our small business philosophy and recommended methods for the mechanics of operating a sustainable enterprise. Accounting is an old study and can be very complex. As a body of knowledge, accounting is rich in nuance and history. The earliest accounting records date back 7,000 years to the Assyrians in Mesopotamia. We do our best in the following section to speak in English and not Greek.

We mentioned that the integration of these concepts and principles can be fashioned to become a "guidance system" for you individually and for your firm.This is your opportunity to craft your own personal guidance system. What key indicators will you rely upon? What could be set as criteria for staff taking action to "steer" this vessel?

Seeing Opportunities

Where others see problems, entrepreneurs see unmet needs and opportunity. After identifying an unmet need, it must be reflected upon and analyzed to find the best entry point to begin addressing it.

Optimization begins with observation. Every organization needs a clear aim with an effective series of methods to achieve it. When we see a "problem" we have consciously or unconsciously compared it to what we think it "should" be. We "measure" the results we see and ask ourselves how it might be better. Measurement is one aspect in effective management, but only one. William Edwards Deming 1900 – 1993 is best known for Plan-Do-Check-Act, the PDCA cycle.[1]

Measurement is highly rational observation. After sometimes extensive observation, we begin to reflect, to notice and to focus that attention. This focused attention is analysis. This is the pathway by which we can proceed towards our best creative work!

What is true about your business? Through analysis, you will increase your understanding of "what is." Knowing what is, can lead you to what's next.

1. Deming, W. Edwards. *The Essential Deming: Leadership Principles from the Father of Quality.* New York, NY: McGraw-Hill Companies, 2013.

Build your guidance system to lead you to your destination. What kind of guidance and navigation systems do you depend upon?

Welcome to Your Gymnasium

Welcome to your business gymnasium. Are you surprised to find a modern gym on your "trading galleon?" Some amenities, like satellite guidance, hot showers, and a great kitchen can't be omitted even if historical accuracy is foregone.

At your physical fitness gym, you have free weights, cardio, and weight machines. Here you have exercise and training "equipment" for analysis, systems and communications to build your insights, acumen, stamina, and expertise. Welcome to the gym!

Challenging aerobics and sets of exercises with progressively heavier weights strengthen muscles. The following mental exercises are designed to stimulate healthy brain fitness and keen business insight. After training, you'll be more comfortable with complex business issues. Some people study algebra or Latin to train the mind in new ways of thinking. Training yourself in advanced business methods gives a person perspective when solving other daunting issues. It prepares a person for complexity and ambiguity.

Predicting the Probable

Predict the probable to envision the best. Go to 60,000 feet to get the big picture. Simplify your finances. Next, put your imagination to work.

Some business owners tell me their venture is special and cannot be predicted. "This business is unique," they insist, continuing, "There is no telling what tomorrow will bring!" I invite them to lay out their bank statements for the last three years and look for patterns. Even high variability is predictive. We can always find ways to reduce anomalies and learn lessons from the past to apply to the future.

We alternate looking back then forward. What you have done has created your past results. To create different results, what would you do differently? It all comes down to your customers' needs. How do your methods fulfill your customers' needs better than your competitors? How do you satisfy customers' needs in an effective, efficient way that inspires and rewards staff while leaving the firm with a profit?

Use financial and non-numerical analysis to study your operations and potential.

Initial Financial Analysis

Your first training equipment is a set of financial analysis tools. You start with a very simplified view of your company's financial history. From your past, you will learn how to predict and influence your future.

Get a broad overview of your past and your probable future. You can then predict a better future as a "best case scenario." With your best and probable cases identified, consider what a "worst case scenario" might be. We will look at annual and quarterly time periods as you practice from a 60,000-foot, strategic viewpoint.

After you have become comfortable with quarterly and annual perspectives, you will learn about shorter periods. You can monitor months and if appropriate, weeks. By practicing, you will soon master the concepts.

In the upcoming exercises, you will need your profit and loss (P&L) statements. Gather your last two or three company tax returns. Prepare to view your P&L statements on your accounting software. When instructed, download or hand post the figures into spreadsheets to practice and learn. Open the *Smart Exit™ Companion Workbook* (paper or digital) to the "Initial Financial Analysis" section. Follow the instructions. Enter your figures in each exercise to the best of your knowledge.

With your tax returns and current year accounting, you can get valuable insights by learning about financial ratios and comparing your firm's performance to industry averages and benchmarks. A few of the many important ratios include the quick ratio and profit to sales for example. The quick ratio is obtained by dividing current assets to current liabilities. Total assets can be divided by total liabilities. Profit ratios include gross profit divided by sales or net profit divided by sales. There are many other financial ratios which can be done. Company ratios can be compared to industry averages and benchmarks to evaluate performance.

A benchmark is a standard of excellence used to compare similar businesses. Industry averages are typically lower than benchmarks which are targets to shoot for. Industry averages and benchmarks are standards of measurement for various types of businesses, such as restaurants, construction, and health care or the hundreds of business types outlined in industry code systems. The older Standard Industrial Classification (SIC) has been largely, though not entirely, replaced by the North American Industry Classification System (NAICS) first released in 1997. A step towards comparing your business performance is to determine your firm's NAICS code.

Benchmarks for narrow industries in specific geographic areas are available. Current, reliable industry data may need to be purchased. With your tax returns and current accounting, your revenue, costs and expenses can be analyzed and compared to those of other businesses of the same type. This comparison can point you towards areas which you might expand or reduce to achieve better results. You might increase or reduce advertising, salaries, rent, insurance, for example, to improve revenue and net profit.

Ratio analysis is a fast way to compare expense categories.

Here is a simple example:

Ratio Analysis

Revenue/Expense	Jan Y1	Ratio	Jan Y2	Ratio
Revenue	$100,000	100%	$200,000	100%
Advertising	$5,000	5%	$20,000	10%
Rent	$20,000	20%	$20,000	10%
Salaries	$30,000	30%	$40,000	20%
Total Expenses	$55,000	55%	$80,000	40%
Net Profit	$45,000	45%	$120,000	60%

The ratios of each expense to revenue can give management insight and direction. Advanced software can quickly study complex patterns in your past, comparing them to other similar firms. This software can place an objective dollar value on your business.

If you do this analysis monthly or quarterly you can aim your actions towards the business value you want. There is much involved in valuing a business, but this is one simple objective measure used to monitor a firm's value. Increased value leads to increased net proceeds when the firm is sold. This is a great tool to reach your personal financial income and retirement objectives. Easy to say and read, not necessarily easy to do.

For now, I suggest you refer to Smart-Exit.com and BeCauseBusiness.com for further resources. By gaining a understanding of basic principles, you'll become comfortable when using software to do it for you.

Build a Financial Integrity Culture

Gaining direct experience with analysis fundamentals will assist you in better business thinking. We learn algebra not necessarily to use it, but to train and develop our mental capabilities.

Remember, you are exercising your brain to improve a variety of thinking skills and abilities. You are learning *how* to analyze a business. Perhaps more importantly, we are training you to, in turn, train and mentor your staff and a new leader. For you to exit, you will need to turn your business over to staff and the new leader.

If you sell your business in a "cash deal," the analysis skills you have embedded in your firm's systems will have made your venture easier to operate, more valuable and substantially easier to sell. If you sell on terms, your staff and the new leader will be expected to succeed with your business and make monthly payments to purchase the business from you. You will want them to be very successful, so there is *no chance* of them failing to pay you.

Reduce Your Successor's Risk

Reducing the risk for your successor is good business for both of you. You need to know and be comfortable with analysis, so you can monitor the performance of the business from a distance without your being directly involved in it. Correcting and supporting your staff and your replacement can only be done if you thoroughly understand and can do the analysis yourself. You have bookkeepers and accountants to do routine work. You must understand what and how they work to avoid or quickly correct inevitable errors while safeguarding your firm from embezzlement and incompetence.

Recall in Chapter One, we referred to the risk of your no longer being involved in a business but depending upon payments from it. Build strong financial analysis skills into your systems, and the abilities of your staff and future leader. You will need to monitor their performance and correct them when necessary to build a culture of dependable, sustainable financial management. Your commitment to their success is essential. A combination of trained staff supporting a skilled leader in a culture of integrity and sustainability is perhaps your best insurance for them staying in business *and* successfully completing the purchase agreement with you.

Learn or review the fundamentals. Turn to your accountant and Be Cause Business Resources for a free demonstration of appropriate financial analysis using ratios, industry benchmarks, projections, risk adjustment, what ifs and objective firm valuation. Before seeking business financing for equipment leases, moves to new locations, purchase of property or other major commitments, be sure to get competent strategic, financial and legal counsel.

Profit and Loss Projection

Enter your figures as a simple profit and loss statement on a spreadsheet and predict your probable results for this year. The accounting term "cost of goods sold" is the cost of whatever it is that you sell. This term is frequently shortened to cost of goods or just costs. Abbreviations used are COG or COGS. In some service businesses with no cost of goods, it isn't used. If the cost of goods is very low or intermittent, it is listed as an expense. Expenses are your overhead, i.e., rent, utilities, salaries. Cost of goods fluctuates directly with either your sales or your replenishment of inventory. Changes in expenses don't typically follow sales fluctuations as directly as cost of goods.

To prepare you for the following exercises I want to review two accounting fundamentals: financial statements and timing.

There are two basic financial reports: profit and loss, and balance sheet. The profit and loss, sometimes called the P & L statement, is more widely used by business owners than the balance sheet. That is a problem.

Knowledge and comfort reading both statements are of vital importance if you are to build your business and sell it. Not understanding and not having accurate, current financial statements may well doom you to never effectively removing yourself from daily responsibilities and being able to come and go in your business comfortably.

I say there are two reasons why the profit and loss statement is better understood by many business owners than the balance sheet.

- Before any venture is launched, the entrepreneur's first inkling of a possible opportunity is the mental comparison between a selling price and the production cost. This basic formula is the essence of a P&L.

- The fundamental tax return for proprietorships and partnerships is the P&L, called the Schedule C. The IRS Schedule C is the return for all proprietorships. A balance sheet is not required for proprietorships or partnerships.

The formula for the P&L is: sales minus cost of goods equals gross profit. Then subtract expenses from gross profit for net profit. Profit and loss statements reflect a period of time, such as a year, quarter, month or week.

The balance sheet formula is: assets (everything you own) minus liabilities (everything you owe) equals equity (what your venture is worth according to the accounting.) It's important to note that there can be a significant difference between the equity, which represents "book" value, and a wide variety of possible "street" values. Each represents a different perspective. You'll need a firm understanding of these different valuations of your business to achieve your Smart Exit™ objectives.

The other accounting fundamental to be understood is timing. Sales for a period must be compared to the appropriate costs and expenses which contributed to creating those sales. There are two types of timing in accounting: cash and accrual. A dictionary definition of accrual is "a charge incurred in one accounting period that has not been paid by the end of it." As the name implies, "cash" basis accounting compares the actual cash received during a period with the actual cash disbursed in that period.

Accrual basis compares the "promises" of money due or money owed, not the actual cash. Therefore when you issue an invoice to a customer for work done, the invoice date determines the period of time that sale will be reflected, not the date when you receive payment for that invoice.

Likewise, when you order something and you are billed for it with an invoice that you then need to pay, the date of the invoice you receive will determine the time period when that cost or expense is incurred. The date of your payment of the invoice is less important in accrual basis accounting than the invoice date. Accrual accounting timing is based upon invoice dates, not the date the cash is received or paid.

Both time perspectives are important. Each shows a different aspect of business activity. If a business receives all payments when services are rendered and pays immediately for all purchases, there are no accounts receivable or accounts payable and then there is no difference between the firm's cash basis and accrual basis reports. A sole-proprietor service business with no employees has the least difference between its cash and accrual accounting. As soon as that firm has the first employee, then there would be taxes withheld and consequently payroll taxes payable and a difference between the firm's cash and accrual financial reports.

Today's accounting software, including QuickBooks, allows both perspectives in their reports. The default for QuickBooks reports is accrual basis. In the "Customize Report" window (top left of a Profit & Loss standard report), the "report basis" options of accrual and cash are "radio button" selections with the following statement. "This setting determines how this report calculates income and expenses." (Note – A "radio button" is used on a website form in HTML code. It is an option to select with a circle that when you select it, the circle is filled with a solid black indicator. Radio buttons are also used in computer programs as well as online.)

Experiment with both options to learn the differences and become familiar with why these different timing perspectives are important in your business.

In the exercises that follow, we recommend using "cash basis" reports because we want to highlight cash flow differences. Understanding cash flow is crucial to staying in business. Cash is the lifeblood of business. Run out and you can be out of business. Keeping track of cash on hand now and in the future is crucial to always having adequate cash to operate. Monitoring accrual accounting is a way to predict future cash. When speaking with accountants, banks, and tax preparers, the assumption is that reports are accrual. If you mean cash basis, it's best to specify that to avoid misunderstanding.

By entering your figures in your spreadsheet or the *Smart Exit™ Companion Workbook* cash flow projection chart, you can compare five annual figures for revenue, cost of goods sold, gross profit, expenses, and net profit. You will notice trends and can *guess* the probable figures for later this year. Treat this like a game or puzzle. What annual revenue and net might you generate this year? Sometimes folks are afraid or superstitious that predicting the future can restrict what's possible. I disagree. You are an entrepreneur and by definition, you are looking toward the future. Take a guess, what's your estimate, predict the future based upon your history. This is called trend analysis.

Take into consideration what you know of your customers. What are the market conditions? What are your competitors doing? What new initiatives are you developing? What are these conditions now? What is your hunch? What is your intuition of how you can meet customers' needs in new ways that make this a good year? In this chart, be reasonable, prudent and conservatively optimistic. Put the "probable" numbers in your P&L spreadsheet or the *Smart Exit™ Companion Workbook* cash flow projection chart.

Non-Numerical Analysis

The following are non-numerical ways to analyze your business. Many great business leaders have developed ways to use analysis to determine ways to innovate. Appreciate inquiry, lateral thinking, and lean manufacturing are three of my favorites. A study of these management methodologies will support you in expanding your thinking and help you navigate and explore new horizons.

APPRECIATIVE INQUIRY

In Appreciative inquiry, an organization is a miracle to be embraced rather than a problem to be solved. David Cooperrider of Case Western Reserve University and Suresh Srivastava first coined the phrase after documenting successful firms that focused on what was working best rather than what was "broken."

Cooperrider was a doctoral student at Case Western. A few blocks from the Cleveland campus is the Cleveland Clinic. For more than a decade, the clinic was a place for Case Western graduate students to do research projects. In the 1980s Cooperrider became very excited interviewing physicians working at the clinic. Cooperrider was encouraged by his advisor, Suresh Srivastava, to "put problems aside and focus upon what gave life and vitality to the organization." That approach of searching and supporting for what is "best" instead of fixing what is "broken" has given rise to the approach called "appreciative inquiry."[2]

What in your firm works best? Let's improve that! Nature and economics abound in examples of appreciative inquiry.

Maintaining an attitude of improvement is similar to invention

---

2. David Cooperrider et al., *Appreciative Inquiry Handbook*. Brunswick, OH: Crown Custom Publishing, Inc., 2008.

or innovation. By definition, this is an entrepreneurial approach. How can customer service be further improved? How can new customers be attracted? How can existing customers be served further beyond the goods and services they are accustomed to purchasing? This approach to improvement and betterment is superior to repairing damage as in "problem-solving."

I declare that appreciative inquiry and innovation can create genuine competitive advantage far beyond problem-solving to catch up with competitors. I am not saying that a certain amount of "problem solving" isn't necessary, but our focus for growth is improvement, innovation and appreciative inquiry – How can we improve?

LATERAL THINKING

"Lateral thinking" is a term used to describe indirect and creative reasoning as opposed to traditional step-by-step logic. Edward de Bono coined the term in *New Think: The Use of Lateral Thinking* (1967), and in other works including *Lateral Thinking: The Power of Provocation* (2006). Lateral thinking is the type of dynamic insight used in powerful strategy and innovation. Simple, incremental development restrains one to commodity-like endeavors that, while they may endure and succeed, will only rarely lead to grand new customer service ideas. Think patent-able concepts, insight that leads to brand new services and products. We're looking for exponential growth, like $1 + 1 = 3$.

When facing daunting challenges and intractable problems, use Edward de Bono's proven methods. Creative thinking is a skill which can be learned. Practice and improve your ability to use atypical approaches if you wish to offer alternatives to powerful competitors and expand your customer base.

Learn about "six hat thinking" and Dr. de Bono's examples of bicycles and ladders having advantages over computers and rockets. Positioning a series of numbers in a stack allows for faster addition than randomly arranged numbers. Use "simple" tools and the "arrangement" of issues to produce better results in your thinking and your life. Learning and teaching "thinking" skills improves mental ability and human productivity.

Routine searching for new sources of learning, arts, and discussion can expand our ways of thinking and viewing subjects. Diverse activities, friends, and travel can stimulate new ideas and solutions for our work lives. Too much diversity and complexity can produce chaos. Too little variety results in boredom. Recognizing the need for balanced stimulation is important in a healthy intellectual life. A secondary benefit is the new business ideas which can result.

LEAN MANUFACTURING

Lean manufacturing is an approach to production that strives to maximize product value with the lowest possible effort, cost and overhead. It arose from the Toyota Production System (TPS). The term "lean" as used in business, was coined in the article "Triumph of the Lean Production System" in 1988 by John Krafcik, based upon his MIT Sloan School of Management master's thesis.

The lean manufacturing approach gave rise to many new management methods including "lean office" and "lean accounting," and the entire field of process improvement. From its most simplistic approach, "lean" methods are "common sense" improvements. What "lean" thinking has led to is a revolution in "just-in-time" supply chain inventory supported by continuously improving robotics and nanotechnology. Further innovations include robotic portion control in food service, the drive for zero waste and the selling of byproducts which years ago cost manufacturers to haul away and dispose of.

Collectively, financial and process management tools as outlined above, in combination with strategy, target and budget techniques have been called "profit engineering." There are many management philosophies developed in the last 100+ years. Some conflict. Goals, strategy and action steps, when aggressively pursued in a finance department, can lead to setting profit targets, then striving to achieve them.

A common complaint when an investment firm purchases a highly respected technical firm is that once accountants are "running" a business, the long-standing traditional, professional values are supplanted by profit and stock market quarterly performance.

Another complaint is that large organizations with multiple remote departments begin functioning autonomously giving rise to what's called "silo" thinking. The departments have their own agendas and see the other departments as their competitors for budgeted funds and power.

The accounting department is setting targets and budgets for the firm overall. Meanwhile, the sales department can be pursuing their targets and over in the new product department, research engineers are working to achieve their targets. As organizations develop, management must work together for the entire firm to improve customer satisfaction and generate repeat and referral business. The aim of top management is to keep everyone working as an effective, efficient team.

Organizations Are Learning Machines

Technology, globalization, and demographic shifts are resulting in economic and cultural transformation. Enterprises that do not adapt are collapsing. Google, Facebook, Apple and the flood of innovative startups are tomorrow's new giants. Last year's giant is next year's dinosaur. What we have seen in the last 20 years is just the beginning of a much larger shift which is and will continue to affect all fields of human endeavor.

Enterprises are being forced to keep up or be left behind. Your staff and services must be relevant to the needs of tomorrow's customers. Customers' expectations for service and response time are changing. By focusing on the activity of learning and change we can adapt more easily.

From Analysis to Systems

We have used analysis to look outward at your past numbers and from it, considered possible future scenarios. Now, let's look at our "vessel" and do a more inward consideration. Is this "ship" as seaworthy as it needs to be to face the course we're setting? What are we doing to achieve our aim? Who is doing what, why, when and how?

We have analyzed through observation, reflection, and imagination. Are we running our craft as efficiently as we could? Filling out the tables with accounting data can be a one-person project. Considering the findings and what can be done to achieve objectives is better done as a questioning discussion between several managers. At some point, it's best to involve the entire staff. Engage a facilitator to lead a company meeting to study possible strategy and tactics for the coming months and next year.

I hope there is a team working together for best results. This is a good time for writing your observations, thoughts, and considerations. What is working, what's not and how do you feel about the outcome so far? Take a few minutes to write this up on a note pad or in the "How Smart Are Your Systems" section of the *Smart Exit™ Workbook*.

"Learning disabilities are tragic in children, especially when they go undetected. They are no less tragic in organizations, where they also go largely undetected," Peter Senge reports in The Fifth Discipline: The Art & Practice of the Learning Organization. Senge asks, "Does your organization have a learning disability?" He goes on to discuss "Prisoners of the system, or prisoners of our own thinking?"

Become a better business craftsman. Put more tools in your business toolbox so you can use the proper tools for each circumstance.

Use creativity and innovation to design and implement a world-class organization committed to outstanding customer satisfaction and efficiency. Ask questions and learn more about management methods such as profit engineering and creating a knowledge-based organization. These methods can be used to modernize your organization as you prepare a new leader to confront tomorrow's opportunities and allow you to make a Smart Exit™.

7

CHAPTER 7 - HOW SMART ARE YOUR SYSTEMS?

People-Based or Systems-Based Management?

Organizations can lean toward a people-based or systems-based management approach. If you describe your work processes by the name of the person who performs the tasks, you lean toward being people-based. Job duties are molded to the abilities, skills, and preferences of the individual. Family businesses and those with 10 or fewer employees are frequently operated this way.

If you have developed systems that optimize products and methods to most fully fulfill customer needs, you probably have written procedures, processes, and job descriptions. The unequivocal expectation is that employees will follow the system to maximize output and customer satisfaction. An automated factory with robots is an example of a highly systematized organization.

Typically, systems-based ventures are more sustainable and automatically have a higher business value compared to people-based firms. Systems-based ventures are more productive and profitable. It is easier to train employees, promote staff to be supervisors and transfer leadership duties and ownership in a systems-based venture.

Systems-Based Organizations

A "people-based" business implies a casual organizational style. "Sue does "ABC" and Tom does "XYZ." Instead, develop your organization as a systems-based business. Define work processes. The tasks of each job role are itemized to show how work is accomplished.

In a restaurant, the hostess seats the guests. The waitress takes the order and later serves the meal. The cook and assistants prepare the meals. The dishwasher cleans up the pots, pans and washes dishes. Some employees are cross-trained and can function in multiple roles. If the cook's assistant doesn't come to work, a waitress may be asked to fill in.

Many small businesses suffer from job duties becoming what an employee likes doing, not what the company needs to have done. A conflict in needs can occur when an employee is very good at one part of a job, but not good at another part. Some jobs can be designed around an employee important to the company, but there is a risk. The situation can change over time from acceptable to poor performance. The owner may not notice or not be willing to do what's best for the firm and ultimately the employee. The other employees in the firm do notice and this can ruin morale and degrade the company culture until action must be taken.

Structure in a Systems Organization

What is the workflow? How is value added to your products? When work is performed there is typically resistance. Work, by definition, requires effort and can be difficult. Some work performed may be incomplete or inadequate and must be corrected. Can you reduce the effort in the work and thereby increase quality? How might adding value be done more easily? Reducing resistance lowers costs and overhead.

Through education, training, research and development, work processes can be studied and "best practices" identified. Capturing these best ways can be done in writing with illustrations, photos and possibly video. With a better explanation of the work to be done, new employees can be trained more quickly.

When errors are made, training for the difficult sections can be repeated. Systems, training, and employee activities can be evaluated. The training can be improved for easier understanding. Advanced training can be given to employees ready to be promoted to more challenging positions.

Growing a company is costly and risky. You know this. You have employees. Systematize new employee training to reduce the time before a new person is fully productive in their job. Once successful at an entry level, what advanced training can reduce work difficulty and errors thereby improving productivity, employee satisfaction, and company profitability?

We can define how an organization meets customer needs, adjusting to changes in competition, credit availability, overhead, customer optimism, government policy, and taxes. We can study an organization as it morphs and adjusts to changes in demand, overhead and labor availability.

Job roles can be refined and worn like articles of clothing. Better tools, machines, and computerized robots can greatly improve quality and production standards. Individuals can perform various and multiple roles at different times and places with a uniform performance so each customer experiences the same high-quality service and can come to expect similar high performance regardless of employee or location.

In small firms, each employee typically have multiple "part-time" jobs. Some jobs are done have interlocking procedures. By defining separate "jobs" the firm can train new employees as firms grow or contract. With written descriptions and procedures, employees can refine activities and new employees be evaluated, coached and offered advanced training. Employees can be promoted and develop career advancement in larger groups.

For example, five employees may have 15 job positions. As the firm grows and employees are added, the job positions can be reassigned to new employees so they can concentrate as the volume of work increases. Original employees remain in the positions they are most suited to perform or they are considered for promotion to a supervisor or moved to a new department.

This is what the chains, franchises, and big boxes have done. Have you? If not, you must do it to compete in today's new marketplace. What is a first step in the right direction?

When jobs are performed identically over time, customers come to expect highly specific products and services. You no doubt love a particular meal at a favorite restaurant. You have out of town guests and tell them about this great fish or steak dinner.

You bring your guests to the restaurant with you. You want it prepared just like you've enjoyed over and over. If it is, you are pleased. If it is not, you are probably disappointed. This uniformity of products and services is known as brand reliability. Brand reliability can produce increased customer satisfaction.

We study ways to improve profits in different ways. We keep products the same and innovate methods for high reliability and maximum value with minimal cost and time. We also innovate products and services to offer new things for our customers' needs and wants.

Automated databases, scripts, and protocols allow for more computerized business operations. Robotics and computerized equipment working with digital products can reduce human input in certain businesses. Nevertheless, many service businesses continue to require high touch.

It's been found that if work is too similar or repetitive, after a period of time, some employees become bored. On the other end of the spectrum, if the work is highly changeable, with widely different demands, then quality and performance can suffer. Matching individuals to suitable work for efficiency and a reasonable challenge is a subject we study and teach about in our Be Cause Business courses.

The Mapping Process

This is an introduction to the mapping process. Creativity with no result or product is akin to hallucination. Productive creativity is innovation. To innovate is to introduce something new, like new methods. Manufacturing innovation is experimenting with different ways to produce a better product faster, easier or for less money. Business innovation, likewise, is experimenting with new procedures in your marketing, operations or administration.

How can we get more work done easier, faster and for less money? You are an expert innovator. It was your ability to innovate that allowed you to first identify the business opportunity which led you into this organization. Your innovation abilities have enabled you to adjust to changing business circumstances while continuing to be profitable. As a master innovator, it's time to take a fresh look at your organization. We all develop habits. You and your staff, customers and vendors all have habits.

Remember creative destruction[1] What products, services or processes are no longer performing well? What habits are holding you and your company back? "Keep the best, drop the rest," as an old friend and accountant Jamail McKinley would say.

1. Cox, W. Michael, and Richard Alm. "Creative Destruction." Library of Economics and Liberty. Accessed March 18, 2017. econlib.org/library/Enc/CreativeDestruction.html.

Streamline and make your organization lean and efficient. Search out and eliminate unnecessary duplication to trim waste and inefficiency. Keep your focus upon deepening your customer experience. Finding and solving clients' deepest needs efficiently is the greatest service you can offer. Operating an effective organization that meets customers' needs with respect, ethics and appropriate compensation for all is a noteworthy goal.

Jack Welch's incessant drive to terminate the lowest performing GE employees, products and business units can be contrasted with a broader look at how an organization interacts with its people, community, and the broader environment.

For example, the "triple bottom line" seeks a balance between the company, community, and the planet. John Elkington, a British consultant, first used the term in 1994, arguing that companies should go beyond the traditional profit and loss statement with a measurement of a firm's social responsibility or "people account" and the firm's environmental impact or "planet account." Elkington is famous for his book, *Cannibals With Forks: The Triple Bottom Line of 21st Century Business.*[2]

Other authors have considered Elkington's profit, people, and planet and gone further with ownership, management, and staff, with customers, staff, and community, and other variations. The point remains, the triple bottom line is a business equation which is respectful, ethical, and appropriate.

These are important questions when launching into a mapping

---

2. Elkington, John. *Cannibals with Forks: The Triple Bottom Line of 21st Century Business.* Gabriola Island, BC: New Society Publishers, 1998.

and innovation process. One of the best reasons to map your system is to innovate.

In our Business Navigation process, you define your business so you can optimize it and mentor a successor to become the new leader, allowing you to exit. Establish what your business is and who your customers are. Identified your company's strengths, weaknesses, opportunities, threats and trends (SWOTT).

Mapping Your Systems

Now we will detail what your staff does, how your departments are organized, and begin mapping your operational process. By mapping your processes, innovation will begin to occur naturally.

Consider your operational process and rough out how a particular basic operation occurs in your business. We start with operations (doing) and administration (running) your business because this is where typical small business owners focus their attention.

Some owners struggle, believing they must do things or they won't get done. They are so busy doing, they are not effectively recruiting, training, and managing staff. It takes money, time, and expertise to recruit, train, supervise, and inspire innovation. If revenue is needed to cover business and personal responsibilities, there is precious little time and money to develop staff and methods.

Mapping your business is the first step. Start with operations. Operations are what you know best. You might begin with a new client's first order. Then show the main steps from the order to delivery and fulfillment, payment, and customer satisfaction. Add or refine steps. Begin to map your operational process.

Maintain a keen eye for duplication. Can you see shortcuts or improvements which could make the process easier, faster, more reliable or less expensive in time and resources? Is there waste? Where is it?

In his famous almanac,[3] Benjamin Franklin suggested that avoiding unnecessary costs could be more profitable than an increase in sales. Duplication can be an unnecessary waste of resources. On the other hand, duplication may be a valuable redundancy, such as a second parachute, a second outboard motor or a second generator.

When a new method is tested and compared to an existing operation, both methods can be run with some staff doing the work in different ways. If there is a separation between the workers, say, in two different buildings or cities, and there is a change in supervisors or some other distraction, what was begun as a test can get ingrained and enshrined, becoming "just the way it's done" in each location. The same project in Minnesota and Miami may have very real reasons for why the work is done differently because of climate, for example. Risk and redundancy must be balanced to differentiate between waste and careful planning.

Next, work backward from your new client's first order. How does a typical new client first contact your firm? Is it via your website, phone, email, or a visit? Begin with a sequential list of various

3. Franklin, Benjamin. *Poor Richard's Almanac*. Lexington, KY: Renaissance Classics, 2012.

inputs such as phone, email, US mail, fax and visits leading up to a client's first order.

Your marketing, advertising, promotion, and sales efforts lead to new clients first contacting your firm and placing an order. Outline these marketing actions. How do your advertising and sales contribute to your client's first approach, inquiry and purchase or decline of your offer?

Now, go to the end of the process. Develop how you follow-up with past customers to ask for referrals from satisfied customers. How do you solve problems with unhappy customers you encounter? Build repeat business using your ongoing customer service program. Outline your customer service program.

In the beginning, we asked the rhetorical question: "You may have a smart phone but do you have a smart ship?" Now we ask the question: "How smart is your system?"

Now let's advance your systems. We map systems, processes and methods to gain a clear understanding of what you are now doing to fulfill client expectations. Doing this gives immediate insight and clarifies thinking on your part and that of staff. It directly addresses the need we feel at times to "get organized."

The following is a gentle slope approach to your "guidance system" development with questions to explore and test your ideas. Capture your ideas as you work to navigate, define and develop the systems in your firm.

Processes to Map

Below we offer examples of possible processes for you to experiment mapping.

Let's examine what activities and functions we do in four fundamental organizational functions: doing, running, getting and guiding. "Doing" is operations and "running it" means your administrative functions, "getting" is marketing, and "guiding" is management. Each can have several sub-systems:

Operations (Doing)

- Intake
- Production
- Delivery
- Follow-up

Administration (Running)

- Accounting
- Human Resources
- Information Technology

Marketing (Getting)

- Market planning and research
- Promotion
- Advertising
- Sales

Management (Guiding)

- Strategy

- Planning

- Budgeting

Many of the processes are connected within and across functional boundaries. Budgeting, information technology, and staff training are examples of activities which reach into and have elements residing in multiple areas.

We begin with **operations** because it is that area where business owners spend the most effort, filling customer orders to maintain cash flow and keep bills paid. We then go to **administration** because after operations, it's in the accounting and banking that the funds are managed. These two areas are most familiar to owners. Communicating your company's brand and value proposition to customers, prospects and the broader community is **marketing**. The area of business least focused upon by small and family businesses is **management**. As management skills are developed awareness about the purpose and goal of the business should increase.. If management processes are developed, it will improve marketing efforts. Good marketing arises out of clear management targets.

"Throughput" is the flow of inputs and outputs that constitute a process. Think factory assembly line. Raw materials arrive at one end of the line and workers add effort to create value in a final product which is useful and of greater worth than the raw materials and the wages paid.

Your firm uses forms of marketing to attract prospects to engage with you and discover if your product will fill their need. If they choose to become a customer, you combine raw materials with effort, deliver that product, collect payment and check in with the client later to be sure you achieved customer satisfaction.

Use the example below as a guide to outline your "factory floor" operations.

Examples: Operations (Doing)

INTAKE

- Process new client in, for example, in a medical practice or advertising agency
- Client commits and schedules appointment

PRODUCTION

- Client shows up for appointment
- Client completes paperwork
- Client is interviewed
- Staff determines client needs and prepares a plan

DELIVERY

- Staff implements plan (delivers product and/or service promised)
- Staff collects payment
- Staff re-evaluates client needs after the implementation

FOLLOW-UP

- Staff reviews plan for next steps
- During this process, office bills client

Examples: Administration (Running)

ACCOUNTING

- Bank deposits
- Accounting postings
- Reconciliation
- Invoicing and Accounts Receivable
- Orders, bill payment and Accounts Payable
- Payroll
- Revenue projections
- Cash flow projections
- Cash management controls & planning
- Investment planning and capital budgeting
- Overall company budget with variance and plan adjustments
- Department revenue planning and budgeting

HUMAN RESOURCES

- Job descriptions
- Recruiting talent
- Interviewing and hiring

- Compensation and benefits

- Scheduling

- Training

- Evaluating

- Advanced or further training

INFORMATION TECHNOLOGY

- Computer network

- Software Licenses

- Security and Passwords

- File storage-digital and paper

- Telephone and fax

Examples: Marketing (Getting)

Prepare periodic (annual, quarterly, monthly) marketing plans. We will prepare an annual strategy with annual and quarterly targets during the Management Process. From the strategy you have developed, begin your marketing plan. Ask what you would have to achieve quarterly to achieve your annual goals.

fFrom the quarterly perspective, what monthly and weekly actions will be necessary to achieve your quarterly targets? Use the following list as a starting point to identify those important objectives for this planning process. (Many of these key performance indicators inter-relate with analysis and planning for the entire company. See management section above.)

MARKET PLANNING AND RESEARCH

- Review history and achievements in previous period
- Describe changes in clientele, competition, and marketplace
- Outline firms initiatives to lead or adjust to external marketplace

PROMOTION

- Anticipate opportunities and how strengths will overcome threats
- Vendor promotional campaign participation (co-op if available)
- Project management
- Merchandising

ADVERTISING

- Goal setting for next periods
- Align clientele with media and brand message
- Plan advertising media to department revenue goals

SALES

- Repeat customer sales – increase average sale amount and frequency
- Former customers – reach out and re-activate dormant accounts
- New customer – identify and approach new customer with existing products/services

- Competitors' market – offer advantages for customers to move business to our firm.

Examples: Management (Guiding)

STRATEGY

- Key person succession
- Exit plans for key persons and stockholders
- Termination
- Recommendations of former employees
- Insurance: key person, liability, umbrella
- Theft and dishonesty policies
- Privacy policies for clients and employees
- Intellectual property management
- Information technology (IT)
- Platforms, computers, networks, tablets, and smartphones

PLANNING

- Risk Management
- Cash management
- Security, password protection, redundancy and back-up
- Communications among the team and beyond
- Client, prospect and community communications
- Website, blog, social media, intranet, video, training

- Databases: customer resource management (CRM), knowledge management

BUDGETING

- Goals and Targets for revenue, net profit and company value
- New product development – R & D
- Communications: Internal and External brand development
- Staff advanced training
- Possible acquisitions
- Technology, infrastructure and capital improvements

Annual Strategic Plan

- Review history and achievements in previous year and quarters
- Describe changes in clientele, competition, and marketplace
- Outline firm's initiatives to lead or adjust to external marketplace
- Anticipate opportunities and how strengths will overcome threats
- Goal setting for next periods
- Projects management
- Department plans
- Quarterly Plans
- Period goals

- Recent history

- Action steps

- Department plans

Monthly Action Plans

- Period goals

- Recent history

- Action steps

Weekly Action Plans

- Period goals

- Recent history

- Action steps

These are suggested sub-systems to use as ideas for you to develop ones that best fit your business. Systems vary from industry-to-industry and between competing firms innovating new ways to capture business and fulfill customers' order profitably. Despite significant variations between manufacturing, professional firms, restaurants and software firms, for example, insights can be gained by considering these categories and your categories, brainstorming and experimenting.

Shannon Brodie, of Business Design Corporation, points out in her courses on organization management that the categories of management and administration are more highly similar between industries and firms than are marketing and operations.

Marketing varies much more between industries and firms. Operations vary the most not only between industries but also between firms. Operational variations can represent key distinctions between competitors. As such, these differences can be competitive advantages. It is operations/marketing methods which most directly differentiate one firm from another fighting for the same client's interest, attention, and purchases. Culture and branding are expressed by the methods, values, attitudes, and approaches of a firm in what is done and how. Think Apple, Microsoft, Dell and Intel.

Let's begin converting your process outline into work plans with specific action steps. Looking at your process map, identify one work plan for each of the four main business functions. Let's start with your marketing efforts, or getting the business.

We will work together here to get started. Resume your mapping process begun in Chapter 5 – "Mapping Your System" with your first work plan responding to a client inquiry or taking an order from a client. Building a work plan is a three-step process: title, objective, and steps. This is the Touchstone job description method created by Business Design Corporation, Santa Clara, CA.

Start with a title for the work plan such as "Client Inquiry." Keep it to five words or less. Now write a one-sentence descriptive objective of 25 words or less. Next, write a series of individual short steps in twelve words or less.

Here's an example:

Step 1 – Title

• Client Inquiry

Step 2 – Objective

• Determine the client's needs and decide if you can meet them; then lead the client from their needs and their desired outcome to make a purchase.

Step 3 – Steps

1. Client contacts us by phone with questions.
2. Take the client's name and contact information, repeating it to the client. For example, "This is (your first name). What's your name?"
3. Ask, "May I have your number in the event we're disconnected?"
4. Repeat client questions to be sure you understand and the client knows you understand their questions.
5. Ask client additional questions if needed to be sure you have determined their needs.
6. Decide for yourself if or which of our products best fits the client's need.
7. Answer client questions indicating how your product exactly fits their need.
8. Determine value to the client if their need is met and compare the client value with the price of our product.
9. Ask the closing question and say nothing further, waiting for the client's response.

10. Answer client objections until the client is certain our product is the best solution to their need.

11. If the client declines, make a plan to get additional information about the client's problem and promise to call the client with a better possible solution (unless it is obvious we can't fill the client's needs).

12. Move to take the order or if declined, schedule a follow-up as appropriate.

Work plans with 15-20 steps may need to be broken into two work plans to keep from getting too complicated.

Now look at the operations function of your business. Once you have the client's order, how do you go about fulfilling it? Write a work plan for filling an order once it is received. Follow the work plan three-step method: title, objective, steps.

Business Navigation Mapping Exercise

Begin mapping your major business processes with your basic operations. For example 1) Customer calls on phone . . . 2) A customer comes into shop . . . 3) Customer purchases or orders, you deliver and are paid . . .

Once you have the list of tasks required for filling the order, write a work plan for one of the tasks required for running your business. This is the administration of your firm. Administration includes the accounting functions like bills, payroll, inventory and ordering; human resources work such as hiring, training and when necessary, firing. Other important parts of administration include securing insurance to reduce risk and maintaining your computer and network systems. Last, we'll look at guiding the business or management and planning, budgeting, and strategy.

The dance between client sales, order fulfillment, staff payroll and cash flow must result in a cash surplus for your reserve account and personal income. Building a reserve account must accompany low personal cash needs or you are doomed to a manic cash flow roller coaster. Write a plan for routine review of finances, making projections, and the other Business Navigation tools to set goals, evaluate results and adjust the goals and actions for the next time period.

Note: In this chapter we've described a firm's main functions in two ways: 1) Doing, Running, Getting, and Guiding and used more traditional names like 2) Operations, Administration, Marketing, and Management. Use terms that resonate with you and your company culture. Design this to support and empower your customers, your team, your values and your vision; make it a comfortable fit that invigorates and resonates.

Develop and use a guiding system, dashboard or scorecard to watch and measure your firm's progress. A dashboard of key performance indicators will assist you in achieving profit, equity, and your business value targets. If you wish to Exit Smart, you must develop a business that is so desirable it "glistens in the sunlight." End up with the retirement account balance you desire and need by substantiating your asking price with a commensurate business value. It's a combination of your assets versus debt, revenue, margins, net, equity those objective measures plus your "secret sauce" that make your business stand away from competitors to your customers and employees. And sets your firm apart from others when finding a buyer to transfer the great business you've built!

Keep track of your industry; read trade journals and blogs. Establish networks of industry leaders, vendors, association and regulatory executives, and competitors in different markets. Keep your ear to the ground and listen, watch to anticipate trends and developments. As president of your firm, it's your job to have the time and resources to meet with key clients and build strategic alliances.

You must know your clients' changing needs before they can articulate them so you have new products to introduce as they become aware they may need them. Lead your market, don't follow your competitors or you won't stay in business.

You can charge a premium for innovation. Guard your intellectual properties, registering copyrights, trademarks, and patents. The alternative is to hustle commodities and fight for the scraps and leftovers. That's no way to build your brand or equity.

What do you appreciate in products you enjoy? How smart can you create your system to be? Clever, remarkable and unique solutions to recognizable situations catch people's attention. They decide to remember it. They mention your firm or product to friends. Everyone wants improvement in their lives. We have come to expect it and we seek it out in listening to news and entertainment.

Articulating specific values your customers enjoy will attract others to you. To be competitive and profitable in today's market, you must distinguish your products and company from competitors to a greater degree than in the past.

Support Genuine Innovation

Have you built a process of innovation into your business system?

By innovation, I don't mean mere invention... When I say innovation, I'm talking about progress. I'm talking about growth. I'm talking about the essential element every successful organization needs not just to survive, but to thrive. If you're doing it like everyone else, you're not innovating.... I put innovation at the pinnacle of economic performance because, without it, we are idle. With it, we achieve great success." So says Gary Shapiro in his book, *Ninja Innovation*,[4] going on to identify three types of innovation:

EVOLUTIONARY

- Improvement competitors and customers expect, such as ever faster computers.

REVOLUTIONARY

- Improvement competitors and customers don't expect, such as smartphones.

DISRUPTIVE

- Unexpected improvement serving new customer values and ultimately creating a brand new market which competitors don't initially understand and struggle to adapt to.

4. Shapiro, Gary. *Ninja Innovation*. New York, NY: HarperCollins, 2013.

Innovation can be considered as either potential or actual. Ralph Stacey, in *Complexity and Creativity in Organizations*, describes potential innovation as altering one's 'schema;' changing one's "perception or model of current primary tasks or their manner of performance."[5] Actual innovation is when that "alteration is beneficial..." Other authors have used the term "creativity" to do things differently in unique and novel ways, versus "innovation" when those creative ways become genuinely useful.

The study and explanation of originality, genius, creativity, imagination, and innovation have gone through dramatic development from the 1700's Industrial Revolution with the stream of inventions arising from the spinning wheel, mills, and machinery. Robert S. Albert and Mark A. Runco in their article *A History of Research on Creativity* assert that "Thomas Hobbes (1588-1679) was the first major figure to recognize how important imagination was in human thought and planning and how constructive it could be. This idea reappeared as a starting point of discussions during the Enlightenment. Learn more about Thomas Hobbes in the book *Handbook of Creativity*.[6]

The management activities described above represent your business command center. In biology, the management command center is the brain.

5. Stacey, Ralph D. *Complexity and Creativity in Organizations*. San Francisco, CA: Barrett-Koehler Publishers, Inc., 1996.
6. Albert, Robert S. and Mark A. Runco. "A History of Research on Creativity" article in book *Handbook of Creativity* edited by Sternberg, Robert J., Cambridge, United Kingdom, Cambridge University Press, 1999.

Business Navigation – Value Proposition

What enhancements do you add to your core product and are they crucial?

How do your competitors add value?

Which do your clients demand, like, or are indifferent about?

What are your clients' associated needs, deeper needs or next needs that if provided, would increase their satisfaction and delight and further distinguish you from your competitors?

How might you reorganize your value delivery to reduce time, effort and costs while increasing customer delight?

8

CHAPTER 8 - YOUR MOST VALUABLE ASSET

————————

Your Most Valuable, and Challenging Resource

Your people, the human resources, are your most valuable asset. Simon Sinek says in his book *Start With Why*,[1] that Herb Kelleher, head of Southwest Airlines was considered a heretic for positing that employees are more important than stockholders. He said, "If you have the right employees they treat their customers right and they come back, buy again, and tell their friends. The stockholders like that."

Some types of business are more labor intensive than others. Regardless, all businesses require someone performing work.

1. Sinek, Simon. *Start With Why*. New York: Penguin Group, 2009.

Vending machines costing $5,000 and up and robotic assembly line devices costing a million both require restocking and service by people.

You, as CEO, can improve your customers' experience by improving your human resources system. First, write it out, and then improve it – your want ads, scripts, and processes for interviewing, hiring, training and evaluating staff. If your compensation plan is well thought out, carefully written and thoughtfully communicated, it will improve your company culture, staff morale, and effectiveness.

If you wish to minimize employee theft and maximize accountability, leaders need to model the behaviors they are looking for with their own speech and actions.

Staff members in firms of your size frequently perform multiple job roles. This allows the staff to grow and shrink as the company encounters varying economic circumstances. As demand and revenue grow, new hires can be trained in these doubled-up job positions. Original staff can then be considered for promotion. Having multiple jobs defined individually allows job position development in preparation for expansion.

Employment Philosophy

What is your employment philosophy? Are you parental, autocratic, or democratic? What is your firm's approach to staff? How do the owner, stockholders, managers and staff relate to each other? The old "command and control" military–like autocratic style has been out-of-date for years. Changing contemporary values, four generations of workers, and demand for self-motivated staff have resulted in a more democratic work environment.

Management styles have evolved over time. Clearly expressed duties, with minimum job performance standards, written instructions for workers supplements hands-on training. A thought-out training program can accelerate new employee competency. Clear expectations can reduce costly hiring mistakes and turnover.

An employee's direct supervisor who is supportive, provides clear expectations, reasonable training, and useful evaluations for further training is a major contributor toward the maintenance of employee productivity and morale. Learn more from Marcus Buckingham and Curt Coffman in the best-selling book, *First Break All the Rules,* New York, NY: Simon Schuster, 1999.

Eliminate the Guesswork

You can eliminate the guesswork by emphasizing teamwork. Teams can do what one or two individuals can't. A team consciousness is crucial. Teams are multiple minds trained to work as one. Learn and then teach staff how to take control and steer your business through stormy seas by using financial analysis, systematizing your business processes, and improving communication within the company and with customers.

Build a resilient, self-motivated, self-managing team that loves serving customers regardless of whether you are present or not.

This isn't a dream. This can be done. Build a strong team, not a dependent team looking to you for all the answers.

Now is the time to gather your team and work together on this Business Navigation program. Set about the work of improving your firm's values and culture. Step away from organizational dysfunction and make your group steady and strong. Written systems in the form of processes, methods, and best practices are a sure way to begin.

If you need help, don't delay. Get the assistance needed that will fit into your new written budget. We show you how in Part Three.

Linking Activities to Positions

By linking activities to job positions we create highly functional job descriptions. Broadly describe the end result of a department or job. What is the desired result? In general terms, describe the activity of the person responsible for producing that result. Then list each significant activity and build a work plan as described above with a Title, Objective, and Steps.

Once key work plans have been drafted, put job titles on your organization chart. Develop an organizational chart representing your current venture and another for what you foresee in the coming year or two, perhaps the end of your next fiscal year. Draw out the job positions you have now on one and what you anticipate on the other. Once job positions are listed, connect the work plans to each job position with a paragraph or two describing the position and its specific responsibilities and authorities. Indicate how work flows from each position to the others.

In both organization charts, place an employee name by each job position. You might indicate the percent of the time each employee will focus upon a particular job position. Scheduling employee time for each job position can reveal if your plan is unrealistic and needs to be changed. An employee's performance, authority, and responsibility must work for each person and the overall team with whom that person works. Schedules must work week after week, month after month considering seasonal variations. Your staffing must be sustainable; if not, it must be changed.

There are free and low-cost methods of making the material available for staff development using Google Drive, PBWorks, Zoho, MindJet, Touchstone, Toms Planner and apps like WorkFlowy. These are platforms for defining processes, work plans and linking them to job titles to create a working environment where best practices can stay current. With Touchstone, work plans can be linked to job titles from either the organizational chart or the processes. Touchstone can also create a checklist from a work plan. (Be Cause Business Resources supports the Touchstone system as developed by Business Design Corporation. The Touchstone system offers many HR management features.)

Business Navigation – Evaluate & Act!

Each key area of the company demands the attention of the business owner

- What is the focus of your attention?

- Estimate the percentage of your time spent in:

  ○ Operating the business, i.e., operations, customer fulfillment and product/services;

  ○ Marketing the business, i.e., promotion, advertising and sales;

  ○ Administering the business, i.e., finance, human resources and cash management;

  ○ Managing the business, i.e., strategy, budgeting and planning.

- Do you have written job titles and descriptions for yourself and your employees?

- Draw a quick organizational chart. Use no names, only job titles, real or imagined.

Managing Activities, Not People

Everyone resists being "managed," particularly bright adults searching for ways to be proud of themselves by making meaningful contributions to an organization they respect. Everyone understands that "activities" must be managed to have efficient communications, respectful interaction and productive outcomes.

Sticky notes, memos, conversation and emails can break down when three or more people are working together. Research and select a management platform for your team to work within. Provide training in its use. Management must model its use, making assignments and asking for reports from within the system. Write job descriptions referencing the management system and requiring actions and evaluations from within it.

Require staff to use checklists with work plans to maintain quality. Be sure that steps are not forgotten or skipped. Develop scripts and script outlines so all customers get the same best information consistently regardless of employee, location or date. Develop and refine forms to capture and share information. Write company policies so employees understand what is expected and required. Clear rules work best.

If handled poorly, staff will express concern that if they tell managers exactly what and how they do their job, management will no longer need them personally. There can be strong push back when trust is low and managers ask for detailed written procedures. Stories may circulate of employees writing their functional instructions and then having their work outsourced.

Build upon your ethical staffing history. Focus system development upon your commitment to building the team from within with innovation and shared values. Always seek to demonstrate how individual employee goals for self development and their family well-being can be achieved by their building a strong, healthy firm to provide steady employment with advancement opportunities. Management must model the behaviors they wish their staff to offer to customers, or success will be short-lived.

Evaluate to Inspire

It is crucial for management to be objective and detached enough from operations to take the time on a scheduled basis to evaluate the firm, its functions, processes, staff, and customer satisfaction. Can you find evidence of customer delight and staff enthusiasm? If so, celebrate it and reward your team.

Staff evaluations are best when management can find examples of alignment between an employee's personal goals and values with those of the firm. Determine where an employee is fulfilling written objectives as well as those places where blockages and resistance occur. Use mentoring, coaching, and advanced training to take employees to their next level in the organization. Acknowledge staff members who have achieved job proficiency. Then challenge staff to re-create their positions with innovations which delight customers while driving down effort, time, and costs.

Alternate between a people focus and structure focus when looking for ways to improve and add value for evolving customer needs.

Inventory, Payroll and Overhead

Inventory and staffing needs fluctuate with seasons and trends. Study your overhead and plan the adjustment of discretionary expenses, ranking which expenses must be maintained and which can be varied through your sales year so that you make money every month, every quarter, and hit your targets.

You can't afford to be caught by surprise. If you are, find out why and revamp your strategy, processes, and work plans.

Voyage-by-voyage, port-by-port we move toward our destinations, goals and targets. As leaders we must be strategic and tactical, able to focus upon the urgent and the important.

If you don't know where you are on your growth curve, find out. Then don't ever lose sight of where you are, so you can strive toward continuous improvement in product development, sales performance and net profit with equity growth. You probably can't achieve all of these each quarter but if you have targets you can aim for them.

Building a Mentoring Program

Mentor your managers and teach them to mentor staff. A mentoring program supports a "learning organization" culture. Ongoing self-improvement and talent development are attributes to be applauded and rewarded in an ambitious venture eager to improve customer satisfaction and company performance.

Make organization optimization a staff-wide project, calibrated with numerical and non-numerical metrics. Privately held companies often guard financial statements while public companies do not, or make statements so complex as not to be truly reflective of actual circumstances. You don't need to reveal *all* your numbers, but be proud of production, gross profit, and reductions in overhead. Sharing information with staff builds trust. Informed employees will work harder and take more initiative if they see where they can make a difference. Employees naturally long for job security. Give them avenues to contribute to that possibility. You and staff are united in your desire for stability.

Make a list of skills you'd like to see improved in each supervisor and/or employee if your firm is small. Jot down a note for each that you can elaborate upon later, then speak with them. Ask what skills, knowledge or practice would help them in their job this week and this month. Ask *them* how *you* might make their job easier.

Identify the likely next job this individual could be trained to assume and master. Laying out job succession in line with possible improvements to customer order fulfillment can reduce time to delivery and thereby overhead.

Scheduled company meetings and trainings could involve 20 to 30 minutes for senior staff training and then mentoring less experienced employees. These sessions can result in building a Frequently Asked Questions list.

Written procedures allow for staff to review when needing to accomplish an infrequent process or one new to them. Written procedures and job descriptions allow for productive employee evaluations supported again by ongoing advanced training and mentoring.

If your firm began a mentoring program, what tasks would you see as most important to begin blueprinting and supporting?

Learn more about training and mentoring and how they differ from coaching, counseling and consulting at Wikipedia.

Understanding their differences and areas of overlap allows you to appreciate how personal growth and professional achievement relate. Grasping a spectrum of tools for efficacy allows for development of a knowledge-based and innovation-focused culture. Interpersonal communications and departmental alignment will improve healthy conflict and team rivalry reducing personal fear and turf protectiveness. A highly-dynamic work environment, perceived as fundamentally safe and professional, supports employees risking error and ridicule by testing and experimenting new methods.

Compensation of staff and management is more complex than direct linkage of pay for performance or routine pay increases for length of service. Performance and service longevity are elements for compensation but there are industry, market and competitive factors as well as retirement, vacation, health, ongoing education, disability and other benefits that also can round out a balanced compensation program. We recommend paying staff above average.

Be fair recognizing the value of work done. Avoid an emphasis upon highly-competitive, performance pay which could ferment greed, envy and excess. Great work should be recognized, applauded and paid for, in that order. Business leaders are wise to have periodic consultation with a human resources expert to keep your firm up-to-date with prevailing wisdom on what benefits contribute to a company culture perceived as a desirable employer with fair HR policies. You may want to become known as an "employer of choice" with your staff recommending the best colleagues they encounter to apply to join your firm. Learn more at Glassdoor, Wikipedia and similar websites.

Integration as a River

Do you notice how the way you engage your team influences their enthusiasm and energy in caring for and serving your customers?

When you walk into a high-end retail, art gallery or fine restaurant, you can sense the atmosphere and the people creating it. Are you satisfied with the atmosphere your visitors and customers experience when visiting your organization?

In his work as a psychiatrist and mindfulness expert, Daniel Siegel observes that healthy people exemplify integration while people in distress seem to be stuck in chaos, rigidity, or both. Siegel offers a definition of emotion, calling it a "shift in our state of integration." Health is movement toward greater integration and illness is movement away from it.

Health might be characterized by integration at various levels from our experience as an individual to interpersonal family relationships to our broader community life. Thus we might consider as "healthy," those organizations where the integration is robust and vibrant, from the employees to management, shareholders, customers, vendors and the broader community.

Complexity, systems and self-integration are cited by Siegel as a "scientific foundation for the benefits of integration – a reason integration is a good thing in our lives.... A complex system (such as a cloud in the sky or an organization) is said to regulate its own emergence."

As open systems, we as individuals and organizations, while capable of descending into chaos, are capable of self-organizing. Siegel says a "triangle of well-being, the system of mind, brain, and relationships might be more fully understood in these terms, and we might apply the principles of complexity and integration to creating health across each of these three aspects of our lives."[2]

Thus a way a leader can begin the process of optimizing, planning for succession and in that process move towards your exit from the firm, could be a) the reading of Smart Exit™, b) the gathering of your people and c) organizing your material resources.

You can guide your progress with project management. Practice operating your business as an open system, conscious of resonance with customers, fostering the talent development of staff while seeking and supporting the emergence of a new leader.

You'll navigate ongoing integration as if it were a river, staying in the center of the channel between the riverbanks of chaos on one side and rigidity on the other. Siegel offers that the mathematics of complex systems argue that "a system moving toward complexity is the most stable and adaptive." Thus the combination of chaos and rigidity compared to harmony and flexibility could be a powerful definition of well-being of organizations and people.

You as a veteran business owner, may have reached your personal and business development crest, then again it may still be ahead. Passing leadership to the next generation may be your crowning achievement.

2. Siegel, Daniel J. *Mindsight*. New York, NY: Random House Bantam Books, 2011.

Transition may require changing long-established habits and moving from directing and controlling to mentoring and inspiring. A better understanding of psychology may give you the structure you need to change yourself, so you can identify and empower a new leader and make a graceful exit.

Your People and Departments

How many employees are in your firm?

What are the departments in your business?

How many employees are in each department?

Next position to define and fill that would improve the company most?

A want ad for the position can summarize the work processes. A more detailed description of the job duties can be used in phone and face-to-face employment interviews. When a person is hired, an employment contract can detail the responsibilities and compensation. An employee manual explains working at the firm. The work processes are used in training and are converted to checklists for the employee to guide themselves in their work and in reports to their supervisor.

As employees gain practice and gradual expertise in a position, they can be evaluated and considered for new more advanced positions. New employees can be brought in to fill the positions being vacated. With cross-trained employees, positions can be staffed as needed despite meals, breaks, illness, terminations or days off.

9

CHAPTER 9 - STRATEGIC PLANNING

Improve the Use of Your Brain To Grow Your Business

The frontal lobe of the cerebral cortex is the part of the brain responsible for reasoning, decision-making, and planning. This section of the cortex is the main element in a human's ability to consider cause and effect and future possibilities. It's been called the "control panel" of our personality and ability to communicate. It's located just behind the forehead. We all use strategy because of this important section of the brain.

We plan sequences of events to maximize results. Casual strategy can be the desire to have a great evening with loved ones and friends. So we read reviews of films, plays, events, and concerts.

We consider the venue location, timing, and deliberate whether to go out to dinner or have a great meal at home first before going out. We consider costs, distances, transportation, and parking. We decide to eat at home. We make a grocery list based upon a menu we may first check with friends. On and on it goes. We use strategy to achieve the outcomes we desire.

Your Strategic Framework

How are you using strategy in your venture? To produce better strategy, more powerful strategy, a strategy that leverages resources more effectively, read authors on the subject, play more chess and study game theory. Learn how to use strategic planning to achieve your Smart Exit™ objectives. But finish this sailing adventure first, your Business Navigation exploration for your "Smart Exit™."

In Chapter One, we discussed possible succession and exit circumstances for a broad range of for-profit and non-profit enterprises. Specific strategies for staff development and senior leader succession and exit requirements vary widely with size, enterprise type, and culture. Some develop leaders from within. Others bring in proven professionals from outside.

Regardless, people come and go and your enterprise must prepare for change and transition or suffer loss and confusion. The costs of not preparing force organizations to take preventive action rather than suffer the pain over and over. We learn from mistakes more than from correct action. Can you and your group learn from the errors others have made? Can you and your group learn from the errors you and your group have made?

Here, we introduce traditional strategic planning with the following exercises.

Strategic Framework

My company's:

Vision: This is the big picture view; what do you wish to create which cannot be accomplished in your or any one lifetime?

Mission: This is a less expansive vision; what do you wish to accomplish in a sizable, though fixed, period of time, say 10 years? This is a big project, but one that is achievable.

Purpose: Why do you want to create or accomplish this mission which leads towards your vision?

Values: What are a few of the fundamental beliefs you and your team use as critical guides? These are the values which you deeply believe must not be violated or equivocated while achieving your mission. If these values are compromised, it would critically diminish the success of the mission, even if that mission were achieved.

Project Management Methods

Everyone uses project management methods. Lists, lists, lists! We make "To Do" lists, grocery lists, things-to-bring-on-vacation lists, lists of necessary materials for home building and repairs. Time, time, time! We schedule time for work projects, home projects, lunch meetings, activities for the kids like soccer and music lessons.

We text and email each other, making phone dates because we can't just call someone when the mood strikes. People don't have time to answer many phone calls. They strive to reduce interruptions so they screen calls and let them go to voicemail. Or, they're on a call, about to go into a scheduled meeting or otherwise can't engage at that moment. Goals and targets are implicit and mental. Advancing our organizations in the world today and tomorrow requires advanced project management.

Fundamental concepts of project management include clearly and simply stating the project objective, making a list of necessary resources of materials, labor, cost, and time, breaking the project into steps or stages with necessary resources required to complete each step or stage. Then we compare the resources available to meet the identified needs and the variance between what's needed and what is currently available.

This planning and organization is part of the project and can be scheduled as the complexity of the project increases. Timelines of stages with clear accountability help to make difficult projects more achievable and with lower risk. There are great tools available online including TomsPlanner.com and the Project Management Institute.

What project management methods do you use in your business, i.e. clear written goals, milestones, measurable outcomes, timelines?

> ### You've analyzed, systematized; NOW SAY SOMETHING!
>
> Entrepreneurs are storytellers. What's your story? You've got a story for everyone – one for prospects and another for customers. You've got a story for bankers and another for investors and perhaps a different one for

prospective investors. You've got stories for staff and another one for managers.

If you can't keep your stories straight you've got problems. You may be looking out for bill collectors, out of business soon or worse yet, watching out for the sheriff.

Written stories with substantiated, bank reconciled accounting and budgets have proven most effective if you wish to grow your venture beyond a job with assistants. Single owner-operator businesses have a long tradition, but like a job, if you don't work, you don't get paid. Assistants can't work without you. With a single owner-operator business, your company value is low and you struggle to sell and transition it to someone new.

Your ability to communicate consistent, credible stories about what has been, what is and what will be is your best bet to grow a genuine, sustainable organization that can adapt to customers' changing needs, making and keeping promises to those you serve and those who serve you.

So what's your story? Let's hear it. Better yet, I'd like to read, analyze and discuss that story with you and your team. Share your story with your customers, vendors, your bankers, and others in your industry. You might get the help of a marketing person to assist you in editing your story first.

Trust and reputation are the hallmarks of a story built upon integrity and success.

10

CHAPTER 10 - COMMUNICATIONS

Your Message, Brand and Company Culture

Each person is unique, and so is each firm. Clearly distinguishing what and why your company does what it does has become of great importance. Establishing and expressing your firm's message, its vision and mission, provides customers with a reason to trade with you instead of another company. That company brand identity is also what attracts certain individuals to seek employment and continue working at your firm rather than a competitor.

The values, beliefs, habits and behaviors of a CEO, management team and staff, express themselves in their products and services to become the company's culture and norms. By being aware of

141

this dynamic, a firm can shape that culture, brand, and message to fit a desired ideal customer profile.

Organizing the activities of staff to add value to products and services needed or desired by customers in such a way as to produce a profit is the key to a sustainable venture, one with genuine value. Leadership and ownership of such a company can be transferred from one individual to another, like any other duty can rotate, assuming those persons have the requisite education, training, experience and temperament.

A management method for business excellence demands that leaders:

1. Analyze, setting targets based upon historical trends and opportunities;
2. Systematize, innovating written systems and job descriptions to improve how they serve their clients;
3. And then communicate, marketing their services, products, and reputation to customers and staff.

Let's foster world-class, innovative, culture-building organizations.

Consider your business. You may have many employees or you may be a solo-preneur. You may work with occasional assistance or with a partner, or possibly with a mix of employees with support from contractors and specialized vendors. Regardless of size, can you see your firm as a team of dynamic, creative architect(s), designer(s) and engineer(s) in your specific niche industry? You have invested years of your life and probably every cent you dare into your venture. Treat yourself as a professional, because you are one.

You may see your firm's core competency as flawless execution, but if you are to flourish, your competency must become the routine process of opportunity identification, goal setting, action planning, evaluation, and innovative re-engineering. Defining, training, and refining your team's precise, dedicated action – this is your challenge as their leader. Strive for flawless execution by rigorous practice: preparation, dedicated action, correction, and improvement.

The Marketing Plan

Plan your future. Design the sales and profit for your firm. It is important for sustainable growth to upgrade your finances and systems before expanding your marketing. More businesses fail from growing too quickly than too slowly. Controlled growth should be your aim, not reckless expansion. Then study, practice, and demonstrate profit engineering in your firm.

Capture your work as you proceed. You are continuously clarifying your thinking and that of your group.

Marketing To Your Ideal Customer

My ideal customer is:

The most important need we fulfill for that customer is:

The #1 product and/or service we perform or provide for that ideal customer is:

What are the secondary needs you fulfill and their corresponding products and/or services?

#2 Revenue Stream: The need fulfilled is _____ with

_____ product/service.

#3 Revenue Stream: The need fulfilled is _____ with

_____ product/service.

What is your market forecast for this year and next? What are the factors which lead you to this conclusion?

What is your forecast for the competition and upon what do you base your opinion?

What is the key message for ideal customer Number One's need?

What are your advertising medium alternatives? (You may substitute promotion or outreach for advertising or use each separately, delineating various marketing approaches. Proceed from where your firm is now.)

Advertising medium #1 and why (benefits and detriments):

Advertising medium #2 and why (benefits and detriments):

Advertising medium #3 and why (benefits and detriments):

What other marketing, such as promotions, special pricing, merchandising, social media, signage, display, website, and/or contests, could augment your marketing initiative?

Determine your top three revenue sources. It is time to prioritize them and select the Number One revenue and profit center which you will focus upon this year. This is probably that product or service which has, and you believe, will generate the largest number of gross and net profit dollars. For that Number One revenue stream, identify and describe your ideal customer in as much detail as you can. Fight the urge to generalize; the broader your target, the less likely you will hit it. Learn more about Creating An Ideal Customer Profile.

Marketing To Reach Sales Goals

Build your marketing strategy and budget upon your answers to the following.

Given the points identified above, I believe that if I promote as follows, I will have the greatest chance of maximizing my investment of capital, time and risk:

My measurable goal with this advertising is to achieve –

By (date) –

An encapsulation of my marketing strategy for achievement of this goal is:

Action Plan

Action Steps. What does each marketing step cost and when does it have to be done? For example, action steps might include making a flyer, hiring someone to demo a product in your store, offering home delivery, or having a seasonal sale. What would each step cost and when would you do it?

Action priorities. Which of your action steps comes first, second, third, etc.?

There is a complex correspondence between various interlocking business concepts. Consider first a firm's vision, mission, purpose, and values. Then think of the relationship between the firm's ideal customer's need and the revenue and net profit streams from the sale of products and services. The marketing message(s) communicate the firm's promise to satisfy those customer needs. The resulting fulfillment success or failure contributes to the firm's reputation and resulting market share. The style, grace, and efficiency of the fulfillment efforts also contribute to the company's culture and brand.

Company Culture

Every cluster of people creates a culture by how they relate to themselves and others. Beliefs and meanings result in decisions and in business, customer needs result in employees offering products and services to fulfill demand. The interaction between customers, staff and management has been termed a company's culture. Organizational culture is important to notice and manage.

The owner/CEO must be cognizant of the dominant influence they exert on the attitudes, values, and activities of their venture. Management's beliefs and behaviors and resulting relationships with customers, vendors and employees give rise to a firm's "culture." Professional self-aware management can design workplaces and script employee/customer interaction for optimal customer satisfaction.

A firm's reputation, market share and company culture are elements of "brand management," and it presents infinite opportunities for you to differentiate your company from your competition.

Roy Davis, Umpqua Bank CEO and author of *Leading Through Uncertainty: Umpqua Bank Emerged from the Great Recession Better and Stronger than Ever*[1], says bluntly a firm's culture is its strategy

1. Davis, Roy, Leading Through Uncertainty: Umpqua Bank Emerged from the Great Recession Better and Stronger than Ever, San Francisco, CA: Jossey-Bass, 2014

and its strategy is its culture. Strategist Rick Torben says "A strategy at odds with its culture is doomed. Culture trumps strategy every time – culture eats strategy for breakfast."

Every organization has a culture. Ignore it at your peril. Recognize it and cultivate the culture to support strategic objectives.

Review the following material and we will discuss how and when you might test strategies to address these management circumstances.

Management and Staff Communications

This includes how managers speak to each other and to staff, customers, and vendors when asking or answering questions and giving directions or explanations. It has a major effect on the creation of the culture of an organization. The tone of voice, attitude, and body language are all important. Sarcasm, optimism, stereotyping, and cultural bias are all contributors. Staff and employee meetings are important opportunities for management to model ideal attitudes to improve morale and productivity.

Staff Dissatisfaction and Doubt Vs. Healthy Culture

Recognize alternative cultures and confront organizational doubt. Every organization has water cooler talk, e.g., the mix of attitudes of the majority of employees and possibly sub-contractors or involved vendors and how they speak when management and customers are not present. Some firms use professional shoppers to test staff responses when management is not present. An increasing number of firms record telephone, online, and in-store interactions for security, possible theft, and quality control to monitor customer satisfaction.

Integrate your firm's internal and external communications. For example, the leadership of this firm is committed to the following values in its communications with staff and vendors:

The values we wish to convey in our external communications with customers and our community agree:

Convert your customers into "pro-sumers." Creating pro-sumers requires supporting a culture so advertising promises are fulfilled and customers are delighted. Pro-sumers are customers who have been transformed into zealots for a brand that has completely enchanted and delighted them, like customers of Apple products. Some ways we might increase the level of customer satisfaction with our products could include:

Internal & External Communications

All business communications can be divided into internal and external.

Internal communications are spoken, non-verbal, and written. They also include the unstated and unspoken attitudes and behaviors that the owner(s), management and staff demonstrate, a.k.a., the company's culture. Even some vendors can be considered internal because of long relationships, deep rapport, and trust. What is said about customers, vendors, neighbors of the business, and former employees behind closed doors?

Internal conversation represents the culture of an organization. Every organization has an underbelly, the water cooler talk, the discouraged, disappointed, exhausted voice. This may be the mirror image of your public vision, mission, purpose, and values. Remember Enron and pay attention to the internal talk in your organization.

Your internal communications include your business guidance system. Given the work you've been doing so far, your methods have growing value. Key performance indicators, dashboards, and scorecards are useful, highly efficient information tools to tell you the health of your organization. Like a person's heart rate, body temperature, and blood pressure, they are "markers" to monitor your firm's well-being. Your guidance system is a step beyond mere information about facts representing what was and is now.

The guidance system is your firm's management "app," an algorithm-like system thermostat that will turn the "heat" up when cool and air conditioning on when it's uncomfortably warm.

Until you automate your management methods with sophisticated computers, your guidance system is your quick awareness such as a) sales are slow, send extra staff home, b) if no one is in the warehouse then turn off the lights and turn down the heat, c) weather report is predicting snow, order the radio station to run the winter weather ads promoting windshield scrapers, tire chains and shovels immediately. Train staff what actions to take and when.

Those training and management methods comprise your guidance system.

Expand your thinking of what's possible for your firm.

Beyond your formal employees, there are always others involved in your company: your partner, spouse, parents, children, best friends, and the support team to whom you vent. We must vent our frustrations and resentments, but to have a healthy company, it must be done carefully and respectfully or the illness will grow and get out of hand.

Write an example of a time when you were surprised by hearing something or seeing a behavior that reflected negatively on another company or on YOUR company:

External communications are all the ways the firm speaks to customers, prospects, neighbors, and the larger community. Explicit marketing and advertising constitute only part of your message.

List some ways your firm communicates externally, either explicitly or implicitly.

1.

2.

3.

4.

Consider for a moment, what does the external appearance of your business say about your firm?

What do your sales floor, waiting room, restrooms, and other public spaces say?

Is your showroom a showroom you are proud of?

What does your invoice say about you? What about your order forms, the sales tickets, or receipts you give customers?

How about your email format, Facebook, website, and other electronic communications?

Remember, these are all part of the complete picture that your company presents to the world.

Now let's take a look at who your customers are in greater detail. Looking at your ideal customer, what is their age? Research, then decide and design your firm's "ideal customer." Who is the fundamental decision maker? What is that decision maker's gender, income, and education? Write a few words that describe that specific "ideal customer." Be as specific as you possibly can, i.e., male, 53 years of age, married with three grown children.

What do you do to reach that ideal customer?

Out of all the messages you send, which message communicates best with that particular ideal customer?

How might you expand that success?

Ask your best customers what their community group affiliations are. What secondary groups exist where you have customers or contacts that you might increase?

What are ways you could support such groups and their members and thereby increase your name recognition?

What are some additional ways that you could reach your ideal customer?

Do you sponsor local groups? Examples might include the local high school clubs, college sports teams, or fraternal organizations such as Rotary, Lions or Eagles. Do you buy ads in their programs, banners at their stadium, or sponsor their events? What are other ways you might reach into those groups to expand your customer base? If you buy or support one thing for the local team or event, what second or third event could you support with the same group to deepen your impact with the membership? Maybe you could be an adult advisor or join the group and participate.

Your firm's employees, their relatives, friends, and neighbors belong to groups which can be influenced to look favorably at your firm and what business it is in. What about your friends, relatives, and neighbors, and the groups and clubs to which they belong? Do they know about your business and services?

Thinking about all the messages you project, list one or more thing(s) you could do to improve how your company is seen by your community.

Marketing is much more than just buying an ad and waiting for customers to call. Successful marketing builds upon strong relationships you develop with customers and within your community. Advertising is a one-to-many relationship in which you work to increase customer interest, traffic, and revenue. Selling is generally a one-to-one relationship. Selling takes place after you have reached customers to explore if you can meet their needs.

Before we leave the discussion of internal and external communications, I want to say that when there is a high degree of integration and congruity between your firm's internal and external communications, the power of your message is amplified. People *feel*, experience, and believe your message is genuine and they can trust you and your message.

If you want people to trust you, value and keep your word. When you make a promise, keep that promise or renegotiate if you must. Integrity is your most precious asset. Don't sell it cheaply; don't sell it at all.

Now we are going to look at advertising and how we convey explicit messages designed to get more prospects through the front door.

Adjusting to a Multi-Generation Marketplace

There is no denying that the multi-generation marketplace combined with the rapidly changing technological environment presents many challenges as well as opportunities.

Some of the challenges:

• Significant generational differences exist in the values and buying powers of the three or four age groups currently active in the marketplace.

The Baby Boomer generation has been preparing to retire but recent housing, employment, and investment market turmoil have altered the plans of many. They have either been forced to remain in the workplace or have been forced into premature retirement.

The size of the Baby Boomer generation is huge by comparison to the X-generation. The Net Generation, sometimes called Net Geners, are again a large generation. The X generation is more conservative and less idealistic than either the Baby Boomers or the Net Geners. The Net Geners, sometimes called Millennials, tend to be impatient and want continuous feedback. They are the first generation born into a digital world. See the *Forbes* article, "What Millennials and Older Workers Can Teach Each Other" in the December 13, 2013 issue.

Which generation does your ideal customer fit into? What can you do to target them specifically? Is your ideal customer's generation dying out or taking over the marketplace? What can you do to expand your appeal to different generations of customers?

- Satisfying customer needs profitably is becoming more difficult.

Satisfying customers' needs efficiently so a profit is produced continues to be the unquestioned business fundamental. However, customers' expectations for quality and demand for value, combined with increased competition are making profitable operations more challenging than ever.

These changes are only expected to increase with the expansion of technology, economic volatility, and the evolving values of younger generations of customers and workers.

Marketing 2.0 is driving changes from The Four Ps:Product, Place,

Promotion, and Price, to the ABCDE of Marketing: Anyplace, Brand, Communication, Discovery, and Experience. [2]

Economic turmoil can drive people to save more and spend less. You've seen how consumer confidence affects saving and spending. The mood of the public shifts routinely as events unfold and news stories report. Customers' expectations for value are high. Online customer and professional reviews are available on all services and products. Businesses selling commodities are facing very tight profit margins. Your product needs to include more – more experience, more relationship, more what? to avoid being classified as a commodity.

• Internet shopping, cheap shipping, and globalization, in combination with sophisticated management and marketing methods, are both good and bad.

The upside: We can research solutions, products, vendors and prices like never before. We can read reviews of the products and reliability of suppliers anywhere in the world now, place orders and have our satisfaction guaranteed in many cases. The downside: The greater availability of information and products is terrific, but it also means we must now give our customers more value, more reasons they should order from us. Everyone has more choice of who they will patronize.

Be the best you know how to be. And learn how you can be better. Lifelong learning is a value to commit to practicing. This is an important habit to cultivate in your staff and company culture. How can you stay current in your industry? You can belong to

2. Tapscott, Don. *Grown Up Digital*. New York, NY: McGraw Hill, 2009. Page 212.

---

and be active in professional and trade associations. You can learn about the pioneers and current experts in your field. Read their books, blogs, tweets, websites, newsletters, white papers, and magazines.

Give yourself a set amount of time, say 30 minutes or more weekly for your ongoing professional development, to watch expert videos and read news about product releases and manufacturing processes. Learn how to enroll in their Really Simple Syndication (RSS) feeds. Combine a holiday with talks or conferences on your industry. Invest in your knowledge, training, and practice. Ask questions and comment on blogs and develop personal relationships with experts here and globally. The world is within reach of your phone, tablet, and computer.

When you identify an expert with whom you would like a connection, research people you know who may know the person and ask for an introduction, then begin email correspondence or schedule a brief phone conversation. Social networks are perfect for meeting authors, experts and others with like interests with whom you can exchange ideas and develop your knowledge and resources.

Now that we know some of the challenges ahead, what are some of the traditional methods of advertising that we can utilize? There are billboards, signage, print advertising, coupons, sales and special offers, flyers, radio and television spots, event sponsorship, event production, philanthropy, bulk mail. Can you think of others?

Other traditional methods include public speaking, writing

newspaper columns, employee surveys, customer surveys. Join a Toastmasters International club (Toastmasters.org) and learn how to become comfortable and skilled expressing yourself extemporaneously.

Local newspapers and magazines (both printed and online publications) look for editorial content about specific business interests. Email the editor and make an appointment to discuss the idea. Submit an outline or a short sample article. If one publication declines, go to another one. Establish yourself as a subject matter expert in your industry locally. Position yourself and your business as the "go-to" expert with an opinion.

Periodically, ask customers and staff questions that could improve your policies, procedures for staff, and your product merchandising and communication efforts for customers. Practice with Google surveys online or printed questionnaires where you can use a spreadsheet to tabulate results. Involve your staff in the questions and results and mentor them to take over and continue the practice. Watch YouTube videos to learn how.

Ask your employees (especially those on the front line): What are the clubs and organizations to which they belong personally. What organizations and hobbies are their family members involved in? How about their friends? Ask your best customers in what organizations they are members. How can your products and services, days and hours of operation be adjusted to better serve them?

Ask your customers periodically and routinely about your products, services, and their satisfaction. What do they need or want and how can you improve your products and services to meet their changing needs? What industry information could you provide? How would they like to receive information from you?

Now let's spend some time on the newer forms of advertising. We all know that marketing options have exploded with the Internet and social media. It is still in a period of tremendous experimentation and flux.

Email

Your email address should be associated with your own website, i.e., you@yoururl.com. What is your email software? Is it web-based, like Gmail, Yahoo, Hotmail, or MSN? Or is it a POP 3 such as Microsoft Outlook, Outlook Express or Mozilla's Thunderbird?

Use your URL email name with a powerful web-based platform. Manage your email campaigns so that you can know when or if your mail has been viewed and links followed. Firms that provide email management include:

Campaigner.com,

ConstantContact.com,

iContact.com,

AllClients.com and many others.

Many firms have separate websites for prospects, customers, and different ideal customers or revenue streams.

Open Source Architecture – Experts donate their time to build free or contribution-basis operating systems, software, and applications such as Linux, Mozilla Firefox, OpenOffice.org, LibreOffice.org and many others.

Browsers – Mozilla Firefox, Chrome, Safari and Internet Explorer are a few of the many available.

Building your libraries

Client contacts – your first and most important library

Editorial – paragraphs describing your core products, services, and solutions

Logo – both typographical and symbol

Tagline – slogans both overall and by narrow niches

Graphics – favorite symbols, page treatments for topic introduction and conclusion, company colors consistent with other formats

Photos – photos of you and your firm. Take photos of your staff, your business location inside and out. Take photos showing you and staff working with clients, both formal and casual. Get photos of you giving talks and presentations. Start with photos you and staff take with cameras you own. As you build a photo library, talk with a local professional photographer and begin replacing your snapshots with better ones from a local pro. Their lighting and composition will be obvious improvements. If not, your photos may be acceptable or you may not *have* a good professional.

Videos – Experiment with short and longer clips. Try ultra short 6 seconds clips on Vine.com, or longer 8 seconds ones on Ocho.com. Let these short teasers interest viewers to longer clips of 1 – 90 minutes. Video yourself, your business and experts in your field whom you respect for your website, emails, newsletters, and on screens at your place of business.

Promotions – structure seasonal and product lines for annual or more frequent analysis to look for new opportunities. Periodically, a product or vendor line diminishes either through your customers becoming bored with it, competition, or social-marketplace change. Companies peak and decline. Your department managers and buyers must be ever-vigilant for a dynamic market movement that will affect how customers judge your firm by the vendors you represent and the vendors who represent you.

Management and marketing authors, theorists and strategists – our business community is local and global. We attend local meetings, lectures, and classes while also reading the Wall Street Journal, New York Times, Harvard Business Review, sources at Stanford, Wharton, and many others, on Wall Street and the political stage. Their advice varies and frequently contradicts. Nevertheless, it's your job as leader of your organization to have some familiarity with various approaches and schools of thought.

Other Internet Resources –

Google AdWords Express has no daily advertising budget minimum; regular AdWords requires only an initial commitment of $10 per day which can thereafter be reduced.

Google offers insights and tools to help your business grow. What can you do now to improve your use of new digital media? What is the first step, the second, the third?

Online maps – request your business name on Google, Yahoo, MapQuest.

Reviews from satisfied clients on public maps.

Wiki – a type of web page which accommodates full two-way communications with various levels of security, such as pbworks.com for "online team collaboration."

Twitter.com – short announcements up to 140 characters.

Blog – No minimum or maximum characters for your articles, ideas and opinions, such as WordPress.com and Blogger.com

Wikipedia.com – contribute to wider knowledge by contributing content to enhance your reputation as a subject matter expert.

Online databases – for managing clients, projects, time, bookkeeping and community involvement, such as online project management sites – Zoho.com, Basecamp.com, AceProject.com, Huddle.com, and TomsPlanner.com

Newsletters – stay in touch with your customers and stakeholders.

Online advertising – become knowledgeable about trends and the current shifting state of online advertising.

Ongoing education and training – Success here requires significant human interaction and involvement between students and instructors. Offerings online include massive open online courses (MOOCs), Google's Open Source courseware, MIT.edu. and Udacity.com

Social Media

General Communities such as Facebook. Set up your company page.

Pinterest.com – read a review at PC Magazine. Read Pinterest background on Wikipedia.

Ning.com is an online platform for people to create their own social networks.

Naymz.com is a professional social networking platform that allows users to network with other professionals and manage their online reputation.

YouTube.com is a video-sharing website on which users can upload, share, and view videos. Educational videos are one of the fastest-growing segments of the Internet. Use your camcorder or cell phone to record yourself or staff demonstrating your products and services to inform new customers.

Industry Associations and Communities

LinkedIn.com – A business-related social networking site used for professional networking. What are the professional associations for your industry? Who do you know who is involved in the different groups, both locally and nationally? Many of the issues you face are being discussed by others in your trade. Learn from your colleagues. Webinars, Zoom.com, GoToMeeting.com, and Skype.com allow no-cost sharing anywhere in the world, at any time.

Begin Improving Your Business Today!

Have you been working with your staff in this program? I hope so. If not, now is the time to do it. Discuss these ideas. Talk with your partners and encourage them to read and participate, to engage and align with you.

Part III

Part III - Turn Typhoons into Gentle Swells

Heading Toward Your Home Port!

We have come a long way together in the Smart Exit™ process. You see better the rewards of learning how to improve steering your vessel with a compass and other navigation tools instead of keeping the coastline in sight and dead reckoning. You can appreciate the possibility of a graceful exit and benefits of a healthier investment portfolio.

Next let's consider nurturing and mentoring staff with advanced training out of which one or more new leaders may emerge. Paving stones on that pathway to your Smart Exit™ could make for an easier walk....

CHAPTER 11 - A NEW VANTAGE POINT

Let's Get The Job Done!

"When all is said and done, no matter what you choose for your marketing dollars, no marketing or communication is more powerful than practiced, skillful execution." – Larry Bossidy and Ram Charan, *Execution*

There are marketing experts who might debate this and there is clear evidence of highly promoted products of questionable value selling strongly. However, fads and fashions change quickly. It's unlikely you're preparing a new pop sensation. If you're building a business to last for years that will fund your retirement, focus on quality and delighting your customers instead of glitz.

There is no better marketing tool than word-of-mouth from delighted customers. Research ways to improve your products and services to demonstrate your marketing claims. Stand behind your work and redo it quickly when you make the inevitable mistake.

Your Development Dance

How can you innovate to boost customer satisfaction? What systems can keep your quality consistently high? A relentless drive to anticipate clients' changing needs coupled with continuous product/service/delivery innovation is the best strategy I know.

Innovative, high-quality customer delight differentiates you from competitors, enabling premium pricing and great margins. As you recall, margin is sometimes called gross profit, revenue less cost of goods sold. Innovation, leading to strong margins, can also *possibly* lead to having net profit higher than your industry's norm.

I say possibly because there is a risk of excessive innovation. Development work is heady stuff and it can be intoxicating, leading to financial unconsciousness. Innovation and development expenses must be moderated. Balanced judgment is required in your development dance. Mistakes are costly. Careless enthusiasm wipes out many ventures. Like steady growth, steady innovation builds market share and sustainability.

Planning – budgeting, testing, refining and retesting within financial constraints – can be executed as revenues are generated, allowing further development. The tension between spending to improve revenue or saving to build reserve and retirement accounts is one which leaders in every organization debate. Is this a "good" investment?

Remember, your goal is profit, savings, increasing the value of the business, finding a new leader(s), transferring stock, and gradually exiting to begin new adventures. On the other hand, if you don't spend, you can't grow revenue, profit, and value. Integration of these opposites in a healthy, balanced tension is the solution.

Putting Ideas Into Action

It's one thing to read a book, another to implement the ideas and suggestions. Learning, understanding, and considering is the first stage. If you get to this part in the book and have been doing more than reading, that's great!

If you have only been reading, consider this. Now is the time to go back and begin your analysis, systems, and communications work step-by-step as outlined. Or do those portions which speak to you. If you are called to, try it now.

Doing the unfamiliar with the better-known processes will stretch you. Remember, you as the owner doing this process is the first part. Your mentoring and leading managers and staff in the processes *with* you is the desired state so they can pull work from you. This *is* a book on succession and exit after all.

Smart Exit™ is your guide to effective action. A guide is like a coach who makes suggestions, recommendations and considers alternative courses of action. Each set of actions has a cost and benefit. We must pick tools appropriate to each "job." Sometimes we use a hand tool. It's handy, requires little thought, and there, the "job" is done.

Sometimes we need a power tool. We'll need to find the tool, connect a cord to an outlet or check the battery. Some "jobs" are projects requiring more preparation, as when painting a room, plumbing, or remodeling a kitchen. Experience and expertise allow us to prepare what is "appropriate" for each "job." Too much preparation and it takes hours to accomplish. Too little and we're not satisfied with the results we produce.

An inflection point in mathematics is a point of a curve at which a change in the direction of curvature occurs. In business, an inflection point is a time of significant change in a situation; a turning point. An example in business is the introduction of a new product at just the right moment to prevent a decline as existing product sales are leveling off. I want to use the inflection point concept to consider what "job" or "project" is next in your organization.

A couple points to remember are:

1. All jobs, projects, and actions are parts of a series which, when harmoniously conducted, build momentum.
2. Business owners typically "live and breathe" in their world of business operations. They are relentlessly "in action," going from job-to-job, project-to-project.
3. If this describes you, or if your results aren't what you want or need for your long-term objective of identifying a new leader and making concrete progress on your exit, then I'd say you may be using hand tools when you need power

tools. You may need better planning. You may be locked into an operations mentality.

You may well protest, that there's this "low hanging fruit" you're gathering and *then* you'll take on "that big project." Or worse, you may say, there are these "fires" which, when put out, will enable you to concentrate on that "big project."

There's an old story that if all you do is "put out fires" the fires will never end. Instead, if you work on designing, building and extending the fire suppression system, there won't be many fires in the future.

Typically, when you say "cash flow," the current bank balance, expected cash to be received and upcoming payroll, lease, and promised vendor payments are mentioned. At this point in the conversation, we go back to the need for routine, ongoing strategy, and project management.

Confusion and self-doubt are frequent companions of entrepreneurs when they are alone and exhausted. A structure for fulfillment is required for large, daunting projects. The maxim, "Rome wasn't built in a day," is a reminder that big projects take time and one can only do what is possible.

We need a team or several teams with carefully orchestrated resources and adequate preparation to build bridges and cathedrals. Again, strategy – have you a) defined the objective, b) planned properly for the size and complexity of this project, and c) assembled the HR and materials along a reasonable timeline?

All significant projects require contingency planning for the unexpected. Perspective and patience help when determination and diligence are just not getting the job done. With all four of these virtues, you and your team will succeed.

Now What?

Once you have at least gone through the processes which your curiosity and determination inspire you to accomplish, we are ready for our next climb.

Remember interdependence and integration when you are attempting to balance the dynamic tensions between the dualities you face. Some of these opposing forces include capital and opportunity, marketing and administration, management and operations, doing it yourself and delegating. By combining and reconciling these forces, which appear to be divergent, into a moderated approach, combining the strengths of each while minimizing the weaknesses of either, you will achieve your most effective outcomes.

You have gone through the first level of the analysis, systems, and communications cycle. You are grasping the inter-dependency in systems of vision, mission, strategy, planning, and budgeting which lead to systems, inspiring staff, and crafting internal communications. This internal creative work leads to expression of why your firm does what it does.

Operating a viable organization is complex work: marketing, serving customers, receiving compensation, managing cash flow, payroll, vendors, accounting, taxes, and comparing actual cash flows to your predictions and targets. This is the dance of your "trading galleon," your ship leaving home port, calling on foreign ports, encountering unexpected adventures, calamities, adversity, solving vexing problems, and celebrating successes.

Then on your metaphorical adventure, you return home to re-provision your ship and do it again. On this trip, you are experienced, wiser and better supplied. Perhaps, in future trips, you'll have new ropes and better sails to make that next venture smoother sailing. Have you identified one or more worthy crew members to be trained as new lieutenants? Are there officers to be evaluated as possible captains?

12

CHAPTER 12 - STEADILY GROW VALUE

The Incremental/Transformational Ballet

Steady, measured improvement has been found to be superior to betting the farm on the long-shot, strike-it-rich opportunity. I have met with management teams who seek and generally realize a conservative 4 to 8 percent annual revenue target during times when competitors are realizing double that growth.

They have explained they avoid greater growth spurts in favor of more reliable year after year growth with less net profit disruption from having the growth and contraction pains with a more aggressive approach. Sustainable improvement is the end, not feast and famine.

A continuous or continual improvement process (sometimes called CIP or CI) is one in which an organization seeks ongoing development in its products, services, or processes. This is another truism from W. Edwards Deming whom we spoke of earlier in "Analysis Precedes Innovation."

This improvement can be "incremental" as alluded to in the paragraphs above with steady, conservative revenue growth or breakthrough. Transformational growth occurs when by diligence, coincidence, or being in the right place at the right time, explosive improvement is realized. This is when genuinely new methods, products, or when technology breakthroughs occur. Examples include: the first transistors, graphical interface on the Internet, or smartphones, "Your Development Dance." Deming envisioned systems with process and customer feedback linked to organizational goals. Deming's work has been credited with the Japanese auto industry's rebirth after World War II leading to the Toyota – General Motors duel.

While we frequently think of revenue when we discuss the growth of a venture, for our purposes in Smart Exit™, we want to go beyond revenue to the steady improvement in the value of the organization and the possible revenue stockholders can realize when ownership is transferred. Yes, revenue influences the value of a company, but profit, equity, and market share are other drivers in the value of a firm and its corresponding stock value.

We're not talking about publicly traded firms, so the value of a firm and its stock value can be elusive. And even if we did discuss public firms with audited accounting subject to the scrutiny of the Securities and Exchange Commission, the Generally Accepted

Accounting Principles GAAP is like a 20-lane highway for possible choices of acceptable reporting and determining company equity. Company valuation is the work of analysts and still the actual market price of stocks can swing widely day to day, hour by hour.

No wonder with smaller firms without audited books, there are multiple ways values can be established. It is quite possible there can be considerable variance between different business appraisers. Also, a business can have different values to different potential buyers depending upon other market factors, say competitors versus vendors versus a stranger to the market.

While steady 6-12% annual growth is great for establishing some level of reliable growth, transformational change obviously occurs and with it dramatic market changes. Every firm needs a research and development effort. It should be budgeted and esteemed by top management, alert to possible new transformational product/ service opportunities and aware of the initiatives being prepared by competitors which could devastate your client relationships.

A New Dance

We've been training you to dance on deck while your trading galleon sails in various seas and seasons. You've managed to avoid falling overboard, I hope. In Chapter 1 we discussed risks from death, diagnosis, or exhaustion of key staff in leader/organization dances. Earlier, we considered employment styles such as parental, autocratic, and democratic. Together we have looked at a variety of perspectives to gain insight into the workings of *your* venture.

Your venture, like a ship at sea, is a complete entity, a whole system. As a whole system, it has many sub-systems. There is an intense inter-dependency between these sub-systems, your "whole system," and the many other systems with which yours interacts.

This is a common model we use in nature and business to organize and understand our world. In mathematics, it's called sets and sub-sets. On hard drives, it's folders and sub-folders. In a library, for example, the subject "knowledge" contains science which contains biology, which contains what we know of the human brain. In business, the national economy includes your regional economy, which includes your local economy which includes your business and your financial systems.

We're going to talk about a new dance. This new dance is one of interdependency and integration. Each of your organizational perspectives, like a separate system or sub-system, functions as a "whole." As we mapped your business in Chapter 7, you can consider and work within your marketing, operations, administration and management departments. Under certain circumstances these perspectives function independently, e.g., the jobs salesperson and bookkeeper have duties you've identified.

These departments do not normally function autonomously. Inter-dependency is the term used to describe healthy interaction between individual people, departments, or organizations. The orders the salesperson process are reported to the bookkeeper resulting in the preparation of invoices.

In very large organizations, the term "silo" as in a grain silo, has been used to describe departments which largely operate autonomously. Classic examples are the five military branches or the multiple car brands of General Motors. When these disparate organizations cooperate, as in the Air Force landing Army troops or Buick using Chevrolet engines and components, it's lauded. Examples of *failures* to communicate abound.

By comparison, dependent or co-dependent relationships imply too heavy a reliance of one upon another. With interdependence, we have open communication and negotiation for each to make offers, counteroffers and reach agreements. Dependence can feed subterfuge and manipulation.

In a healthy culture, a salesperson may suggest improvements in procedures to the manager. For example, salespersons may not create an order form *and* an invoice, if it's a cash sale and no invoice will be used to bill. Or, the bookkeeper may ask that the salesperson regularly record on new customers' orders the client's complete contact information such as the client's cell phone and email address.

An organization with an interdependent culture fosters respect for all stakeholders: customers, staff, management, stockholders, and the broader community. Competitors relate in healthy modes as industry colleagues in which there is recognition of the skills of each and when possible, collaboration to meet their industry and customers' larger needs.

Organizational cultures which have become predatory towards

competitors have been sometimes seen as manipulative towards staff or vendors.

Mild cultural aberrations can include the common complaint among some owners and managers, "getting employees to do what they're told." If this is one of your complaints, it might be best for you to transfer ownership of your business quickly, because you may have a larger cultural issue than you understand. This could be a systemic problem, which could be improved, but might become much worse. Dysfunctional organizations can breed embezzlement and multiple forms of abusive or criminal behavior.

Owners and managers work on their company morale and the culture which supports it all day, every day, regardless of whether they know the terms or theories. Astute managers can tell something is amiss when they drive into their parking lot, walk through the door of their shop or call in and hear how the phone is answered.

They "know" how they want their business to "look, sound, and smell." If there's trash in the parking lot, or a sign is crooked in the front window, or they walk through the front door of their bakery and do not smell fresh bread and feel the warmth from the oven, their radar is alerted. They proceed to check everything.

If you call your business and the phone is answered on the fifth ring, followed by a long pause and then the usual greeting, I bet you're going to ask questions and wonder if you're getting an accurate representation of what's happening. True?

We don't want our customers to approach our business and find we're not presenting ourselves professionally. It erodes their confidence in our ability to serve them. Franchises and chains continue to demonstrate to independent organizations the value of consistency. McDonald's food might not be the greatest, but in thousands of world locations, the food is served hot, fast. There's also a high probability the bathrooms are clean and service is courteous. What can your customers count on when approaching *your* organization?

The rate of social change has been accelerating dramatically since World War II. Developments in technology and science are impacting our culture. In turn, there have been human rights advances and demands for a new level of individual respect for people in organizations. The days of ordering employees to "do things" and expect to have a vibrant business interaction in which customers love to do work with your staff are over.

There are two fundamental management approaches to customers and employees: inspiration and manipulation.

Know the Forces Driving Your Firm

Often, there are few significant differences in the products and services offered by competing companies. When there is a new approach, the first mover advantage can be quickly lost as features are copied by competitors. Unless the "first mover" can build a "moat" that delays competitors' entry, and the first mover scales quickly to dominate the market, it is frequently the second or later entrants who avoid the costly mistakes of the first mover and benefit more.

Why do your customers do business with you? Why are your employees your employees? Answer the questions here before reading on for maximum benefit.

Sinek asks these questions. Sinek says most company leaders respond that customers buy from them "because of their superior quality, features, price or service.... In other words, most companies have no clue why their customers are their customers.... If companies don't know why their customers are their customers, they probably also don't know why their employees are their employees...."[1]

If companies don't know why their customers decide upon them and why their employees choose them, then most companies are working from "incomplete, or worse, a completely flawed set of ideas of what is driving their business."

If this is true, then how do companies know how to attract more customers or more employees when they need them? How can they know how to encourage loyalty?

Sinek says that when companies don't know the "why" around their customers and employees, they tend to use manipulation techniques such as price and features. Once customers buy from you based on price, features, or convenience, you have become a commodity to them. When a competitor offers a lower price, a new feature, or becomes more convenient, your customer becomes *their* customer.

As price is driven lower, margins decline. To stay ahead, you will

---

1. Sinek, Simon, *Start With Why*. New York, NY: Penguin Group, 2009.

need to increase volume but that increases overhead which in turn can decrease net profit. Much of today's advertising is a form of manipulation. Companies promote price, features, and convenience because it works, at least for a while.

According to Sinek, by gaining a deeper understanding of why customers buy from you and employees want to work for you, a firm is able to clarify their message to both customers, and employees. The "why" for your firm originates in the limbic brain of you, your customers and your staff. The limbic brain is very wise and has deep knowledge. It is, however, incapable of language. By engaging the cerebral cortex of stakeholders, language can be invented that describes this "why, " this limbic knowing. Then, stakeholders can refine and enhance essential actions and descriptive messages congruent with your core values' identity.

We distinguished earlier that a business cannot be adequately described as a machine using the "clock" model. Organizations can be better understood as living, breathing organisms. Ventures are born, mature, grow old, and die. The lifespan of small ventures is typically a few years. A small fraction of businesses stay in business for 10 years or more. Far fewer can survive being transferred from one owner to the next. Your business functions as a living organism. Your goal is to infuse it with life and transfer leadership and ownership, with you being repaid for your cash and time invested and the resulting company value. I think a brain is a very good model for a business. Can you develop the intelligence and capability of your staff and systems to serve clients effectively and profitably and transfer leadership and finally ownership?

Nurturing Skill and Self-Efficacy

We are striving to make you cognizant of your own nurturing skill and "self-efficacy."

We advocate entrepreneurs know management history and follow trends to discuss new approaches with staff. Experiment and practice the tools we're discussing to cultivate a continuous learning environment and better guide your venture. Train and mentor staff to "steer" the business, and give advanced training and support to a new leader.

These practices will improve your confidence in yourself. Your staff and the leadership candidate will gain greater confidence as their skills and training proceed. You, your leadership candidate, and staff functioning together will improve teamwork skills and confidence in learning and growing.

Your ability to measure the "value" of your business will improve as you experiment and read further into the complexities, strengths, and weaknesses of different valuation methods. I am confident that as you do these things, the actual value of your venture will improve and your venture will be more responsive to the needs of the market in which you operate.

Advanced Tools

Remember "integration as a river." The river banks represent chaos on one side and rigidity on the other, as a metaphor for mental health and disorder as described by Daniel Siegel in *Mindsight*. Consider the multiple areas of your business life in which you can integrate seeming dualities to produce a balanced holistic view of your enterprise. First, practice. Do these business improvement methods yourself. Then discuss and invite your new leader-in-training, and key staff, to consider these concepts. Train and mentoring them. Strive to engage your entire team and company stakeholders.

Routine Analysis

Earlier in the book, we suggested creating simple profit and loss reports for a few years of history and projections for the remainder of this year and next. We worked with annual and quarterly periods.

Now we'll provide you with tools and exercises to zoom out for greater strategic insight and zoom in for a more granular experience with monthly and weekly periods. The ability to zoom in and out gives a perspective that your staff needs to adapt to ever changing, sometimes wildly swinging economic tides, and keep the ship afloat.

Storms, tempests, and hurricanes can occur suddenly, and then overnight we have the sun and calm seas. Preparation and training can turn an otherwise tragedy into just a bad day.

Life is hard. If we train for the worst and make it hard on ourselves, life may not seem quite as hard as if we expect a picnic on deck every afternoon. This book is a training manual. Use it to strengthen the abilities and resolve of your crew.

Advanced Financial Analysis

In the Chapter 6 section titled "Initial Financial Analysis," we encourage practice of quarterly projections for probable, best, and worst case scenarios. Here is your chance to do this monthly to keep closer watch of how each month is leading you toward your quarterly and annual targets. Some industries and firms monitor and project these cash flows weekly during volatile periods or routinely.

Here you enter your monthly revenue, costs of goods sold and expenses for the last two years and the months so far this year and then project the remaining months.

As you do this, your ability to project and predict will improve. With it, you will understand that as you take actions to increase sales or cut costs and overhead you'll simply and clearly see the actual results. This will "ground" your experience in the power of your decisions to improve your checkbook balance and reserve accounts. Take charge *now* of your finances!

Likewise, earlier, we discuss comparing quarter-to-quarter cash balance, expected increases, and declines. Note seasonal variations. Now practice this by month or weekly.

If you operate a restaurant, bar, entertainment, or other venture where weekly fluctuations are substantially influenced by local events or weather you may well need weekly and four week periods for analysis instead of monthly to adequately manage cash and profit.

Using the monthly and quarterly charts, you can predict cash flow by months for a couple of years and by quarters for a longer period. This kind of prediction can substantiate your strategic long-term plans. This financial diligence can improve your self-esteem and confidence. As mentioned earlier, don't hesitate to ask for professional help to get this started or to do it periodically. Turning this from an exercise into routine reality can be difficult. We are available to support your applying these methods until you are completely comfortable doing them and having your staff do them with you, for you and later, you mentoring your future leader to do them.

Also in Chapter 6, "Initial Financial Analysis," I suggested that if you have one or more tax returns and accounting reconciled to your bank accounts, you can have reports run using ratio analysis. Your ratios can be compared to prior years and industry averages.

You can do "what if's" in which you adjust prediction percentages to consider different growth rates and risks. By doing this analysis, say quarterly, management can graphically see the results of actions taken during the previous period and how they either increase or decrease the value of the business and how it compares with its industry.

Advanced Systems Development

You can learn more about financial analysis at www.BeCauseBusiness.com. We have a large library of tools and resources for improving how you organize and process work. We also have access to broad and deep experience in the Institute of Management Consultants.

Your questions and your dilemmas can be addressed to the Be Cause team of professionals or student interns at both the graduate and undergraduate level. Students need "real world" projects for their social change and thesis projects. Putting bright eager minds to work can accelerate an organization in the midst of change and opportunity. Call to find out what and who might be available to help.

Advanced Communications

A facilitator is a consultant trained in the methods of organizational psychology and group dynamics. Facilitators guide company meetings that might otherwise be led by the owner or managers. By working with a facilitator, leaders can select among a variety of processes for one that fits best for the desired outcome and resources available. By having a facilitator, the owner, manager, or "de facto" leader can participate with the team, working with staff to search for solutions and innovation, instead of jockeying between running the meeting and trying to be a member of the team. Contact us for options from a periodic half-day session to off-site weekend retreats. Try something new to create breakthrough results.

Your Strategic Plan for a Successful Exit

A business plan is used to either raise funds from an investor, secure a loan, or as an operating tool to guide the leader in either a start-up or a bold new reshaping of an existing firm.

Strategic plans are used routinely on either a periodic basis as opportunities arise or as a scheduled annual event. I support scheduled strategic work, augmented and updated when great opportunities arise. Maybe a competitor or vendor is interested in selling and makes you an offer you can't refuse. One of the best ways to learn how to sell your firm and step away is to practice how to evaluate and buy a firm. Practice shopping for firms to improve your ability to present your firm for sale.

Your highest priority as owner, board chairman or CEO is crafting strategy or evaluating the strategy your executive staff prepares for you. Updating or crafting a new strategy frequently begins as a private thinking and writing exercise. In his book *Good Strategy, Bad Strategy: The Difference and Why It Matters*, Richard Rumelt has coined the term "kernel" to represent the three parts of a given strategy: diagnosis, guiding policy, and coherent action.[2]

Rumelt cautions against "wish driven strategy in which the desired target is arbitrarily selected and then a strategy developed to achieve it. Instead, he opts for his "kernel" that, like a doctor diagnosing a patient discerns a prognosis and lays out a course of action to heal the patient.

So too, the strategist evaluates the business in its marketplace, considers customers and competitors, and crafts an action plan that, like a lever, gives the firm competitive advantage to better serve the customer's changing needs. From the kernel, "a proximate objective" is to achieve a realizable significant first step.

From the private work of the leader, the team is brought in to

2. Rumelt, Richard. *Good Strategy Bad Strategy: The Difference and Why It Matters.* New York, NY: Crown Publishing, 2011.

develop and engage the strengths of their insights and enthusiasm. It may proceed first with managers and then more broadly to staff and stakeholders with a meeting or facilitated retreat. From the strategic plan, tactical plans are prepared for quarterly, monthly, weekly, or daily specific measurable action steps that define when, by whom, at what cost, and with what budgetary targets.

The Business Navigation work you have done has clarified and developed your thinking in key areas. You and your team can now pull together these elements into a strategic plan. A simple outline for a strategic plan is:

- A brief history of the firm, your staff, products, services, and customers

- The vision, mission, and purpose of your firm

- Why you and your firm do what you do

- Staff development and identification of a new leader whom you can mentor

- Your ideal client now and moving forward

- Your firm's current circumstance and short-term future in terms of customers and finances

- Your strategic 'kernel,' coherent action, and a 'proximate objective' for using your strengths to overcome weaknesses and seize opportunities while avoiding threats

- Your "Plan B" in the marketplace and with your new leader candidate

- Your project management methods to implement that strategy to increase net profit while developing the new leader candidate

- Your prioritized transfer, financial, and exit plan alternatives.

Contact us through Smart-Exit.com for support and coaching.

This has no doubt stimulated a few additional, immediate ideas or questions. Write down your best ideas for mentoring your successor, supporting him or her to improve market share, your company value, and how and when you will exit. What is your ROI dollar and date?

CHAPTER 13 - IDENTIFY LEADER CANDIDATES

Who Wants It Most? Who Is Most Capable?

Using a military analogy, it's as important to build the "unit" in the Navy as it is to identify and train a new lieutenant to possibly become the new captain of your ship. A new leader in a dysfunctional team will probably struggle or fail.

You want to avoid having to find a new leader who, with a fraction of your experience, can do what you've been struggling to do. Improve the functionality of your team with the assistance of the leadership candidate and support the new leader in continuing to improve the team and themselves.

It's hard enough to find someone who can lead a good team. There are far fewer individuals who can do a better job than you have with your years of experience. If you do find that one-in-a-thousand charismatic genius to help you, great. Be careful though, that genius might outsmart you in negotiations or worse, study your venture thoroughly, then build a better one next door to drive you out of business while you're trying to sell and depart. I've seen it happen.

Begin by identifying the values and behavior attributes most crucial for each job position, including department managers and the overall organization leader.

It's been said that attitude is more important than skill. Attitude grows out of our values and as such changes little and slowly. Skills can be more readily taught than attitudes can be imbued. Building a powerful organizational culture can be an incubator and support system for open minded, curious individuals wishing to flourish in a creative, healthy environment doing work which they experience as intrinsically valuable.

Enthusiasm and professionalism are two values I hold in high esteem. Enthusiasm is marked by a general "can-do" willingness to relentlessly serve customers' needs and notice possible improvements to how that service is rendered. The opposite of enthusiasm is pessimism. Positive psychology seeks to reinforce the strengths of healthy, realistic enthusiasm. As mentioned earlier, efficacy is the ability to accomplish objectives. Self-efficacy is a belief in one's own ability to complete tasks and reach goals. You must have this trait to achieve business success. Teach it and mentor self-efficacy in your team and the new leader.

"Professionalism" is having a "greater interest in my clients' well-being than in my own," my dad, Stanley Anderson, would remind me years ago. He stressed repeatedly that we were professionals in our retail travel agency in the 1960s, 70s, and 80s. He was a proud member of the American Society of Travel Agents and emphasized we would offer clients the lowest fares available from which our customers could choose the time of day and other travel factors. We were paid a commission for the travel we booked and while our earnings were lower, having happy repeat customers was a superior business strategy, he would say.

Nurture enthusiasm and professionalism in your firm. Demonstrate it in how you relate to customers, competitors, staff, and all with whom you interact. Your modeling of these values will result in your attracting staff and customers who will treat you and your customers the same. Identify senior employees who model it to new staff members. Staff who model, demonstrate, and teach your core values are the ones you can consider as leadership candidates. Reward these leadership candidates with advanced training. Become keenly aware of their personal values, family circumstances, and career aspirations.

Conduct frequent staff meetings and individual evaluations, praising the values of enthusiasm and professionalism. Give public recognition to staff demonstrating your firm's highest values. Back up the public recognition with additional financial compensation. Praise and reward the values and behaviors you want to see repeated.

Discover who *most* wants to be the new leader. Nurture all who compete and reward appropriately and fairly. Remember, there are two levels of ascendancy: management and stock ownership. There are various ways you can reward staff seeking to build the value of your firm.

At the same time, don't rule out anybody. Don't rule out the quiet bookkeeper in the back room. Don't rule out anybody because you don't think they can afford it. You may be surprised to learn that money may not be an obstacle. Oh, by the way, don't make money an obstacle. You want a new leader who can lead the *company* to make money, so the company can pay you, not necessarily the new leader personally.

Some individuals who can express their interest and desire to lead may have less genuine leadership capabilities than another person who doesn't express themselves verbally or demonstratively but has superb instincts and capabilities. It's your job to find the *best* new leader.

As an organization grows, the opportunities for management positions and organization officer positions and shareholder ownership increase. This allows for multiple "leaders." It's been found that a single CEO reporting to a board with a single board chairperson, leads to improved performance compared to consensus or unanimous decision-making. Individual responsibility and authority can produce exemplary results.

Ultimately, you are looking for a replacement CEO to manage daily operations. Over time, this person, perhaps with or without others, will purchase your stock as you step away from the business.

While I refer to stock ownership as in a corporation, in an LLC it is units and a percentage of the partnership, and in a non-profit, ownership can be either the group's membership or the community-at-large.

Who Can "Be" and "Do"

The trick in a Smart Exit™ is to become what you've wanted to be all your life. It can come suddenly or gradually, but you notice you now ARE BEING what you have wanted to become. It is and has been becoming a reality and now, it simply is. This could be a function of maturity, self-actualization as Maslow described it, or just the realization that *IT* wasn't quite as difficult or distant as it had felt for many years.

Like most good "tricks," this one has several interlocking pieces. How the pieces fit together is what makes it a "trick." A next piece, then, is that as your metamorphosis is occurring, you can be conscious enough of the process to demonstrate what and how you decide and take actions with staff, customers, and your leadership candidate.

As Sinek points out, if you can become very clear about "why" then other things fall into place. The magic of an exit is it requires a summation, a consideration of the whole. In that process of understanding the beginning, middle, and conclusion, a why, or "the why" for you, for customers, for staff, for everyone, can come into stark relief. There can be an "aha" understanding for you and others around you and that clarity can fire the imagination of staff and the leadership candidate.

You need to "get it" or "grok it" or the Italian word "capisce" or "capeesh." What is the why, the "it" that's gotten you out of bed daily for years, to go and do this "whatever?" Fill in the blanks. "Oh, but it's just a ... print shop, restaurant, dry cleaners, whatever...." I don't "buy it." I think it's been more than that for you. Instead, it may be the impression etched into your psyche many years ago in which you saw something in beautiful work. You witnessed your family, or saw happy customers after a great meal at a diner. You observed someone really well dressed in a freshly pressed starched shirt feeling proud and capable.

What Was *That Vision?*

When you can stay connected to "that vision," why you are passionate about seeing your customers experience something like it, you can better inspire and lead staff instead of just "telling them what to do."

Independent ventures today are the progeny of the craftsman – apprentice, teacher, student or master/chela relationship, but without the centuries of abuse. As such, independent business is as much art as science.

Returning to our nautical theme, you are the captain of your ship and you have a crew. Who among your crew has the confidence, the ability, the enthusiasm, the interest, and commitment to inspire customers and other aspiring employees? Which of those qualities, if they are missing, can you spur into being?

You are nurturing, encouraging and developing the entire staff. Which of them has been, and is demonstrating a willingness or the most curiosity to learn and excel? This may be your candidate or one of your officer candidates from whom you'll select the new leader.

Can these officer candidates act and reflect upon their actions, the why they are doing what they do? Can they "be" and "do?"

What Are the Risks?

There are a multitude of risks, of course. Risks and complaints run the gamut:

- Your sales and profits are flat or declining and despite efforts, there's nothing you know how to do to increase either.

- You have exhausted savings and the survival of the business is at stake.

- Your customers' needs and wants are changing or competition has increased and you are struggling to adjust and adapt.

- Your candidate doesn't understand the responsibilities, feels inadequate, and has self-doubt.

- Someone in the candidate's family is holding the candidate back with fear.

- Incidents arise in the candidate's personal life, accidents, or illness for the candidate or close relatives which affect the candidate's ability to be present and responsible. (The Truck, Diagnosis, etc. from Chapter 1.)

- You struggle to inspire staff for a variety of reasons, perhaps because you "just have a business to sell" and don't understand your "why" beyond supporting yourself and your family.

- You are exhausted and can't muster the enthusiasm to re-invent yourself and your business.

Yeah, yeah, life is tough. OK, but you have to do *something*. You must choose and then take consistent prudent actions. Focus is required to get you from where you are right now, to your "next step" toward that Smart Exit™. So what's it going to be?

Get a coach. Search out a new perspective. Clean up and improve your business. Print out your tax returns and some financial statements to review. Build a three-ring binder with dividers. Write up your strategic plan with your tactics and action steps and put them in the binder. Look over your recent ads and promotions.

Write up your marketing and promotional plan and budget. Put them in the binder. Engage your team and coach to work with you to achieve together what you can't do alone. Make a budget and projections. Compare actual revenue and net to your projections. Write down what you are learning and assign staff to come up with better plans.

What can you do over the next 90 days, or the next season, that will boost sales? Look at your overhead. How and from whom are you buying? What can you do to improve your gross and net profits? You'd wash your truck and change the oil before advertising it for sale, right? If you're selling your house, I'm sure you'd fix the broken gate and put on a fresh coat of paint to dress it up.

Having a Plan B

The best Plan B is proceeding to move towards your Exit while nurturing and enhancing several key business elements, including:

- The value of your business in general

- The ability of your staff to operate without your direct daily involvement

- Your staff's conscious awareness of adapting to clients' changing needs

- Your staff's ability to understand the broader overall market, competition and how technological, economic, and environmental changes are now and will continue to influence your customers' needs and your ability to fulfill them profitably

- The leadership abilities of your managers

- A single leader who is demonstrating abilities and interests in a way that inspires customers and other employees.

If your business culture is healthy and your systems are strong and vibrantly able to adapt to change, your staff will be in position for a capable leader from inside or outside the firm to take over from you. Plan B is the continuous improvement of your firm and staff. Then, if one leader candidate doesn't work out, another can be found.

If the firm is sick and staff is weak, then finding a new leader is a different kind of problem. Go back to Chapter 1 and begin again. In teaching this material as the Business Navigation 101 class, it is typical for entrepreneurs to repeat the program several times. Each time, their business grows stronger.

14

CHAPTER 14 - ADVANCED STAFF TRAINING

What Serves Your Customer Best?

If you want a "Smart Exit™," you must build and refine your Smart Team™.

You want to turn your business over to a leader who has vision, initiative, and keeps his/her promises. You want that leader and his or her team to be responsible and responsive to customers, their interests, and needs. This type of company culture takes careful nurturing on your part, backed up with advanced training and ongoing mentoring.

Think continuous training for continuous improvement. The Japanese term is "zazen" and it's been a driving factor in the growth of the Asian auto manufacturers since the 1980s resulting in the struggle by US automakers not to be overpowered.

Describe the current interaction between your most valued customers and your staff. How can the interaction be characterized?

Defining the duties of each job position and how you will train new employees to execute those responsibilities is crucial to your customers consistently being well served. What new product lines or services will you need to satisfy their changing needs as well as acquire new customers? What is your plan to achieve your goals? Traverse the distance from today to tomorrow. Detail your job position as president and the job positions of your staff as explained earlier.

Can you describe some other styles of business culture which you could consider or test for your organization? If you were to "automate" your venture more, how might that impact your business culture? For example, a significant online marketing campaign such as Google AdWords, supported by a shopping cart and fulfillment house could dramatically change a typical bookstore into an Amazon.com-like venture. What is on the horizon of your ability to envision and imagine your future for 5, 15 or 25 years from now?

Take your work processes, and one-by-one, describe your training using the Touchstone and Taylor Protocols job description methods. The Touchstone job description is elaborated in Chapters 7 and 8 – "Four Business Functions." The Touchstone approach typically leads to practical step-by-step, recipe-like job descriptions. In the Taylor Protocols' approach to job descriptions, the most important question to ask is: What is the "contribution" to a customer made by this job position? The contribution is the "why" of the employee's actions. The employee's exact tasks are the "how."

First, blueprint the Touchstone and Taylor approaches to your employee's job. Then, define the training activities and time required for each step that enables the employee to perform the job satisfactorily. Studying and improving the training will inform and improve the description of the job itself and vice versa.

In crafting your management methods in the Touchstone or similar software, you can outline different valuation methods for varying stages of business sophistication.

By using Taylor's Core Values Index assessments with staff and job descriptions, you'll identify staff or vendors best able to assist you with annual company value estimates according to the management methods used.

As we've mentioned earlier, the value of a business can vary widely based upon who would own it, marketplace circumstances, and possible transfer terms. Before a new stockholder/leader has been identified, a business value can be established by a business appraiser for several thousand dollars or based upon estimates using formulas in specific settings. Once a year that abstract, objective value can be reviewed and adjusted, giving you a figure you can compare against prior years and one to improve next year. Conversations with accountants, bankers, various insurance/commercial real estate brokers and others in your industry can improve your ability to value your firm. It's worth repeating: Shopping to buy other firms like yours will also improve your ability to value and prepare your business for transfer.

In this way, your confidence and ability to "steer" your value upward with the help of staff should also improve. Of course, you must remember that value can be greatly influenced by a) terms and b) changeable markets and c) ultimately rests upon the agreement of a willing seller and buyer. Practicing valuing and improving the value of your venture can mean more money in your retirement account and if you train your next leader well, less risk in the future for you and the next leader.

Staff Achieving Personal "Why"

What are the personal goals of your staff and how can you inspire staff them to see that they can achieve their personal life goals by advancing and reaching the company's values and goals?

For example, use of quality human assessments can assist the culture of organizations. Greater self-awareness in members of management and staff facilitates communications, which in turn can improve customer communications and customer satisfaction. Value alignment between individual employees and the organization's values can aid employees in seeing that they can achieve their own personal goals by helping the firm achieve its goals. When staff members more clearly understand their own personal values and goals, frank conversations with management in periodic evaluations can lead to improved staff performance.

There are over 2,300 human assessments in use. The Myers-Briggs

Type Indicator arose from theories proposed by Carl Jung in his book "Psychological Types'" published in 1921. Jung's ideas were developed during World War II by Katharine Cook Briggs and her daughter Isabel Briggs Myers and published in 1962.

Psychologist Robert Hogan has developed a comprehensive method for considering personality, leadership, and organizational behavior. Personality is quite changeable and scores on assessments are subject to change.

Lynn Taylor of Taylor Protocols is a turn-around business consultant who has built an assessment system around a person's core values, based upon Jung's work. Core values change less and more slowly than personality. Taylor Protocols has developed a Core Values Index assessment which can be taken online in 10 minutes or less and is quite reliable for establishing deep personal preferences which can indicate cultural fit between individuals, types of work activities, and the teams in which they work. Be Cause Business Resources staff have training in the Core Values Index and support the work of Taylor Protocols, Inc. Lynn Taylor is author of several books about Core Values.[2]

Becoming All They Envision

Do you support your staff becoming all they can envision? In the 1700's, Rousseau advanced the concept of human "perfectibility" in the classic 1762 treatise, *Emile, Or On Education*. During the French Revolution, this book inspired a new national education system for France that has influenced the western world.

1. Jung, Carl. *Psychological Types*. Princeton, NJ: Princeton University Press, 1971.
2. Taylor, Lynn. *Core Values Handbook*. Tukwilla, WA: Elliott Bay Publishing, Inc., 2010 and *The Grass Is Greener*. 2011.

Humankind is gradually evolving socially from a survival mentality to cooperative families/communities and chosen careers.The success of our species can be attributed to our social natures and our ability to work together.

Slavery and serfdom and employment have led to contractual agreements and team models such as self-organizing and open-source. These advanced organizational models in which one's time and skills are exchanged for payment, access to sophisticated resources, additional training and introductions are ways we are learning to support each other in achieving all we can envision for ourselves.

Neuroplasticity is supplanting the limitations of a "hard-wired" brain. The more liberal pragmatic idealism of the "what's possible" entrepreneurial philosophy is overcoming the more conservative "what's in it for me" or "every man for himself" philosophy.

The concept of progress is comparatively new historically, decidedly Western, and particularly American. The idea that we can improve ourselves gives us the ability to inspire staff to improve themselves. Together, you and your staff can devise improved systems which provide desired services and products delivered to customers efficiently and profitably. The system and staff can be nurtured as the organization's culture is refined so you have a dependable business model that operates as employees come and go. More importantly, in this operating system, you can learn to give advanced training opportunities to staff, identify a new leader, mentor that leader and staff to move forward, purchasing the venture from you so you can make a Smart Exit™.

15

CHAPTER 15 - SELL "RIGHT" FOR YOUR SMART EXIT™

Selling Alternatives

In all circumstances, you must determine what your business is worth. Determining business value is more complex than valuing real estate. Typically, there are several values that can be established and a single value is chosen or determined from the range of value approaches.

Valuation methods can vary depending upon the industry as well as its stage of organization. A newly organized firm may have an office, equipment, and inventory with little revenue, much less profit. In this case, what is the value of the assets less liabilities? The accounting balance sheet equity may be close to its street value. Even in this situation, if this firm is in a highly dynamic industry niche and has possible "first mover" or "early mover" status, has big name talent with deep pocket resources, pedigree education, and high power connections as investors, advisors or contracted management, then the value can be many times the "book" value.

If the firm has average or higher than average revenue, then the revenue may be useful as a multiplier in conjunction with balance sheet equity. A more mature firm with revenue *and* net profit can in turn use profit as a multiplier in the value formula.

Examples of industry factors include how Facebook, Twitter, LinkedIn, and other famous websites use unique visits. Retail drug stores use the value of each prescription times $5 to $10, and print publications use the number of paid subscriptions or advertising contracts. The basis of value is what is most prized and sought after by leading firms in your industry.

Business values involving revenue and net relate directly from the IRS 1120 corporate and Schedule C proprietorship tax returns and the quality of the accounting which is their basis. Obviously, if there is a hint of duplicity in the accounting, a wise buyer will only consider the purchase of assets and want nothing to do with corporation stock which might later be subject to an unfavorable IRS or state revenue department audit for improper sales tax or employment reporting.

Like a classic auto in near showroom condition or a new "big hit" market mover, only the very finest businesses are attractive enough to be sold via stock transfer to discerning investors. Polish the chrome and oil the decks on your sailing galleon to make it shine and shimmer in the light.

As we said earlier, much of this work you do alone. In the best of circumstances, your staff and your leader candidate will contribute substantially. It is wisest if you engage a business consultant or coach with specific experience and expertise in succession and exit work. Your accountant will be deeply involved in the process. There are tax considerations with different sale alternatives that must be fit to the exact needs of yourself, your business, and the buyer.

You will need an attorney to craft agreements that are clear and definitive. You want a win/win agreement to maximize your gain with minimized risks. You will talk with your insurance agent to cover a variety of risks including key person, employee dishonesty, health, disability, and an umbrella for unnamed coverage. Keeping your investment counselor up-to-date will be important for your retirement and estate planning. The consultant or coach will function as a general contractor does, seeing that all the moving parts synchronize while you keep growing the business and mentoring your candidate.

You may sell to a stranger or transfer to a key employee or family member. There are particular pros and cons of each alternative.

Pick your candidate. Study the person's abilities and personal resources. With assistance from your consultant and input from your accountant, consider two or three ways you might transfer ownership to the candidate in ways that work for you both.

Typically with a stranger, you may receive a larger down payment or it may be bank financed, or paid in full in cash. A cash deal usually results in a lower sales price and lower risk. If you don't structure the purchase correctly you can suffer dramatically higher taxes. You must work with your accountant around your individual tax circumstances to know what form of payment is best for you.

The safest general way to accept cash is for a direct deposit into a retirement account. Retirement accounts are the safest way to hold cash as they are beyond the reach of creditors and even the IRS so long as the gains have been legally earned. There are different retirement accounts: some accept before-tax dollars like traditional IRAs. ROTH IRAs accept after-tax dollars. Meet with your tax planner to determine your best alternatives. Then, negotiate with your buyer to achieve that specific outcome.

I have a colleague of mine who has securities licenses and is an accountant. He has studied the federal tax code, passed professional IRS examinations, and is what's called an enrolled agent. He is recognized as an accounting and tax professional by the IRS. He creates custom fit transfer packages to benefit business sellers and buyers. If the seller owns the building housing his business and wants to sell the business, one way is with a "1031 Exchange" whereby the gain from the real estate sale can be passed forward into a new commercial property with no immediate tax to be paid. This is an example of the many creative approaches to business transfer.

Examples of Business Sales

A former client with whom I was no longer involved, sold a popular restaurant at a Florida resort city, receiving all the sale features he asked for but he suffered a significant loss because of poor tax planning.

There are advantages to selling to a strategic or financial buyer for cash or bank financing as mentioned, and there are advantages to selling to a key employee or family member.

In either case, preparing your business properly can result in higher net proceeds to you. One advantage of carrying the note is the likelihood of a higher sales price, interest income, and possibly a lower tax burden, assuming you have an exit advisor and tax accountant with deep experience transferring businesses. Good for you. It can also enable someone to own their own business that otherwise might never have had the opportunity. Good for them. That's a win/win.

An oral surgeon client and friend met a newly graduated oral surgeon and told him of his practice and his interest in retirement. They worked out a contract in which the new surgeon worked for the older doctor for one year. Then the retiring surgeon worked for the new doctor. At the end of the second year, the retiring surgeon stepped away. This was a very smooth and successful transfer for both of them, for the staff, for the business as a whole, and ultimately, for their customers.

This oral surgeon went from full-time surgery to part-time allowing him to invest time and money in other ventures. One of the other ventures was a dental insurance company board of directors on which he served. He helped to bring that firm to sales exceeding $100,000,000, then retired from board activities. By retiring from full-time work as a surgeon in his early 50s instead of his 60s, he's authored books, begun a retreat center and contributed to many, many other people's lives far beyond being a dentist and oral surgeon.

A pharmacist client purchased an independent drug store early in his career. He began to think of retirement. He hired a pharmacist working in a local hospital with the verbal agreement that he'd retire and sell his store to her. She worked a couple of years as a pharmacist next to him. Then he made her head pharmacist for a year. The next year, he made her store manager and the following year he sold the business to her. She bought a pharmacy doing almost $4 million annually that was worth $1 million, for $3,000 cash down and the promise to keep the pharmacy profitable and buy back his stock in the corporation. Once substantial stock is purchased, she'll begin purchase of the building. Who would have thought that she could buy a million dollar business with $3,000 in cash? There are creative solutions for every possible business transaction. Don't dismiss a potential leader because, on the surface, they don't appear able to afford it.

If you haven't already, begin some initial conversations with the candidate you have identified, mentioning your general plans to retire "sometime in the ____ future." (Fill in the blank appropriately for your and the candidate's situation.)

There are critics of company presidents and majority stockholders who are more focused on their personal wealth than the company future, employee well-being, and the interests of customers. Some Initial Purchase Offerings (IPOs) and cash buyouts from Wall Street and Silicon Valley have provided us with ample evidence of greed and abuse of corporate power.

Despite occasional extremes, abuses and excess, balanced plans and efforts to care for your mental and physical well-being and that of your family and business team is of great importance to your future, both individually and that of your broader community.

There are important reasons to have employment agreements with key employees. One is to provide for fair compensation to them while working and in retirement because if it weren't for dedicated professional staff, you'd a very small business and little retirement income. A second important reason is to reduce the chance of staff members holding the seller hostage by threatening to resign if not paid a bonus when the business ownership changes. Careful agreement development is important as it could change the "at will" employment status in certain states. Consult your attorney. This book is general business information for your education. Nothing herein should be construed as legal or tax advice. Consult your professional team for questions about your specific situation, or contact Be Cause Business.

Employment versus Stockholder Status

In micro and small businesses with annual revenue below $10 million and less than 15 – 30 employees, the main stockholder is typically the CEO. This may not be true if the organization is poised for growth, but generally smaller firms are run by the owner or majority stockholder.

It is useful to emphasize that employment and stockholder duties and responsibilities are distinctly different, though there can be some overlap, particularly in smaller ventures.

Typically, when an attorney assists a proprietorship to become a corporation or LLC, the corporation bylaws or LLC operating agreement is a boilerplate template designed for a single owner or husband and wife. Frequently attorneys will recommend a single stockholder even when a husband and wife are involved depending upon the level of involvement of the spouse, whether one or both come to him for counsel and are operating in a community property state or not. Consult your attorney or we can introduce you to attorneys who are expert in business transfers.

The provisions in the bylaws or operating agreement for single or husband and wife stockholders are naturally heavily weighted toward the original and/or majority stockholder so that the attorney may easily defend that client in the event of a lawsuit. If stock is given to employees, family members, or sold, the rights of the minority stockholder are essentially "at the pleasure" and complete choice of the majority stockholder.

Being Board Chairman

The goal is to have a competent company president to guide day-to-day and week-to-week decisions. The staff is experienced and motivated to satisfy and anticipate customers' changing interests, needs, and wants. You can craft a small board of directors to begin in earnest the work you've been striving to do for years, to lay out a direction and plans for the company to achieve the vision you had for it years ago when you began. You can consider the capital improvements you had to put off for either lack of time or cash.

At this point, you can establish a list of management priorities with the new president and to some extent with input from the department managers and staff with rising talent who have imagination and can see the potential.

Your board can be casual or more formal. It may be you and the new president or you may invite your accountant, attorney, banker, investment or business advisors. You may meet quarterly or just once or twice a year. You can do an annual retreat over a weekend or have a meeting to discuss issues, then have dinner or drinks with spouses and friends. It's your board. You can develop it as it works best.

One of the annual assignments for the stockholders can be to review and update the valuation model with current year data, make prudent projections, and vote to establish the current company value for the next year. In the event of a need by any stockholder to liquidate some or all stock, you have all agreed on a recent figure. In the event an emergency or opportunity arises, and more than a year has transpired, then the last value applies.

This method gives stockholders the incentive to check that value formulation routinely and always keep it fresh and agreed upon. In the event of some dynamic change affecting value, an emergency meeting and valuation can be held between annual meetings.

If one stockholder offers to purchase stock from another at a price other than the last agreed upon value, it can be the right of the other stockholder to counter offer to purchase at that same price. Terms of purchase must be thoughtfully prepared and all stockholders must maintain enough cash and near liquid reserves to be able to make a purchase or fend off a purchase. This need to maintain significant cash can impede the growth of the firm or add to its stability.

Carefully written operating agreements and bylaws respecting all stockholders are of crucial concern for healthy ongoing stockholder relationships.

On the board's agenda should be a routine look at company policies which will influence the procedures the president, managers, and staff implement. There is a body of knowledge about board development. Your bylaws, operating agreement, and agenda items will guide the way the board functions to achieve the targets and goals which you and the president see as important and possible. Small businesses with a board of directors can keep a strategic perspective on the long-term goals of the firm.

By contributing your time and efforts on these higher level management initiatives, you are mentoring your new president and now his/her team to fortify their management ability. This advanced training can pay great dividends to all. They need confidence that they can adapt to inevitable change, operating efficiently and profitably regardless of how markets may evolve.

You want security that they can continue to grow in their personal and business capacity and that the president and firm will keep their commitments to the stream of payments promised to you.

Smart Exit™ and the *Companion Workbook* are built upon the precept that writing our plans and ideas can lead to clearer thinking, better decisions and well thought out conversations that lead to skillful execution. Thinking by itself accomplishes nothing. Plans must be put into action. Results must be evaluated and future plans amended. This is a practice which has no end. Model these behaviors and recognize the accomplishments of others.

Their success is your success. Their future is your future.

This is the time to review your work and tie up loose ends. What additional steps do you see by which you are going to make your "Smart Exit™" to a new venture, a new team or more family time, travel and fun? Can you imagine? I hope so....

We are in sight of our Business Navigation destination. *Hooray! Yippee! Yikes....*

You are coming into *your home port*.

As we pull into the harbor, reflect upon our adventure together. Like organizing your vacation photos, go back over your Business Navigation insights. Polish, refine and gather these jewels you've collected, your inklings, plans, and next steps.

In the past, we would get film developed and assemble the photos in albums. More recently, the photos we take on our smartphone are sent to family, friends, or posted on our social media sites.

Sometimes we make slide shows, maybe with some favorite music. Like coming home from an extended international adventure, assemble your insights into something you can use and continuously improve: your strategic optimization, succession, and exit plan. This will form the basis for your next grand escape from an otherwise dull routine.

Take your Business Navigation jewels as a new understanding to share with partners, staff, colleagues, and friends. Flawless execution is a practice that has no destination. This is a good time to plan and envision your *next* adventure.

We look forward to your suggestions and ideas for how we can improve the Smart Exit™ adventure for others who will follow. We sincerely want your feedback on the work we have done here together.

We're interested in your odyssey crafting and carrying out the plans you are making and implementing. Write us a review with your suggestions for the concepts we've laid out. We grow from your comments and criticism.

You've been the leader of your organization for years.

What new projects *beyond* the firm are awaiting you?

Do you have a new great idea? Is it a new firm or travel, family, and fun?

Are you ramping up for a new challenge or is your biggest challenge reshaping what you've built so you can move on?

By reading, *and implementing* this book you will learn how to:

Grow the value of your business,

Identify and mentor a successor,

Sell the business to the new leader, and

Make your Exit Smart!

Good luck and God Speed!

New Adventures To Consider

Strategic Planning: Insight to Action

Right Person, Right Job: Improving Staff Productivity

Optimization Strategy Tune Up

Project Management Methods

Book your next passage at BeCauseBusiness.com and Smart-Exit.com

What are your questions?

Contribute to the participant forum at www.BeNavigator.com. Learn from other participants and assist them in their learning.

Questions, concerns, observations, suggestions....

Call the Be Cause Team at 800.249.1622

Good luck with your venture and adventure. We are here to help.

Resources

Learn more about Business Navigation, watch video, listen to podcasts – Join the Be Cause Community.

Notes and References

Below is a partial list of books and resources drawn on in the writing of this book. For further information call 800-249-1622 or visit Smart-Exit.com and BeCauseBusiness.com

Albert, Robert S. and Mark A. Runco in article "Handbook of Creativity" in *Handbook of Creativity*, edited by Robert J. Sternberg, Cambridge University Press, Cambridge, UK 1999

Aulet, Bill – *Disciplined Entrepreneurship: 24 Steps to a Successful Startup*, John Wiley & Sons, Inc. Hoboken, NJ 2013

Bolman, Lee G. and Terrance E. Deal, *Reframing Organizations: Artistry, Choice and Leadership* Third Edition Jossey-Bass, San Francisco 2003

Deming, W. Edward – statistician and consultant, is misquoted as saying, You can't manage what you don't measure. A Wikipedia article points out that running a company on figures alone is one of seven deadly sins of management.

Digg.com, CNN.com, trade journals

Gerber, Michael E. – *The E-Myth Revisited: Why most small businesses don't work and what to do about it*, HarperCollins, 1995, 268 pages. Read review.

Lipman, Frederick D. – *The Family Business Guide: Everything You Need to Know to Manage Your Business from Legal Planning to Business Strategies*, 2010

Valuing Your Business: Strategies to Maximize the Sale Price, 2007

The Complete Guide to Valuing and Selling Your Business: A Step-by-Step Guide to Selling and Ensuring the Maximum Sale Value of Your Business, 2001

How Much Is Your Business Worth? A Step-by-Step Guide to Selling and Ensuring the Maximum Sale Value of Your Business, Prima Publishing, Rocklin, CA 1996

Kornfield, Jack Ph.D and Daniel J. Siegel, MD – *Mindfulness and the Brain: A professional training in the Science & Practice of Meditative Awareness*

Osterwalder, Alexander and Yves Pigneur – *Business Model Generation: A Handbook for Visionaries, Game Changers, and Challengers* John Wiley & Sons, Inc. Hoboken, NJ 2010

Value Proposition Design: How to Create Products and Services Customers Want, John Wiley & Sons, Inc. Hoboken, NJ 2014

Ries, Eric – *The Lean Startup: How Today's Entrepreneurs Use Continuous Innovation to Create Radically Successful Businesses*, Crown Publishing Random House, New York, NY 2011

Really Simple Syndication (RSS) Industry News Feeds

Rose, Hilary and Steven Rose – *Genes, Cells and Brains*, Verso Books, London UK and Brooklyn, NY 2012

Senge, Peter – *The Fifth Discipline: The Art & Practice of the Learning Organization*, Doubleday, New York, NY 1990 and 2006

Shapiro, Gary – *Ninja Innovation: The Ten Killer Strategies of the World's Most Successful Businesses*, HarperCollins Publishers, New York, NY 2013

Siegel M.D., Daniel J., *Mindsight*, Bantam Books – Random House Inc., New York, NY 2011

Sinek, Simon – *Start With Why: How Great Leaders Inspire Everyone To Take Action*, Penguin Group, New York, NY 2009

Stacey, Ralph D., *Complexity and Creativity in Organizations*, Berrett-Koehler Publishers, Inc. San Francisco, CA 1996

Wolfe, Norman – *The Living Organization: Transforming Business to Create Extraordinary Results*, Quantum Leaders Publishing, Irvine, CA 2011

Twin 25 Year Old Brothers Accused of Attempted Murder of 70-year-old father who was difficult to live with and work for – Bledsoe & Sons Gutters and Sheet Metal, according to The Daily Record, Ellensburg, WA September 18, 2013

Glossary

A/B versus multivariate testing Most commonly used to evaluate websites for popularity and usage. A/B is testing which of two choices is chosen more and multivariate offers multiple options. These tests can be used for all sorts of alternative evaluations to compare methods.

Balance sheet One of the two fundamental financial statements; shows assets less liabilities equals equity.

Best practices Methods which have been proven to produce optimal results.

Exit plan The strategy by which an owner leaves a company with the company continuing successfully under the supervision of a new owner with the original owner adequately compensated for his investment of time and money.

Financial statements There are two fundamental financial statements: the income statement and the balance sheet.

Income statement One of the two fundamental financial statements; shows revenue, cost of goods, gross profit, expenses, and net profit. Sometimes called the profit and loss statement or P and L.

Key Performance Indicators KPI is a set of measurements used to determine the health of an organization

Key person succession The strategy for training staff to advance and take over responsibilities from current leaders.

Margin Another term for gross profit on an income statement.

Profit engineering Designing and operating a business to consistently reach preset profit targets.

Systems In business, a set of practices which result in desired outcomes.

Further Reading

Brown, John H., How To Run Your Business So You Can Leave It In Style, Business Enterprise Institute, Golden, CO 2006

Bossidy, Larry and Charan, Ram, Execution: The Discipline of Getting Things Done, Crown Publishing Group, New York, NY 2002

Buckman, Robert H., Building A Knowledge-Driven Organization, McGraw-Hill, New York 2004

Gerber, Michael, E-Myth Revisited: Why most small businesses don't work and what to do about it, HarperCollins, New York 1995

Johnson, H. Thomas and Broms, Anders, Profit Beyond Measure: Extraordinary Results through Attention to Work and People, Free Press Simon & Schuster, Inc. New York 2000

Johnson, Larry and Phillips, Bob, Absolute Honesty: Building a Corporate Culture that Values Straight Talk and Rewards Integrity, American Management Association, New York 2003

Kegan, Robert and Lahey, Lisa Laskow, How the Way We Talk Can Change the Way We Work, Josey-Bass, San Francisco 2001

Kohn, Alfie, Punished By Rewards: The Trouble with Gold Stars, Incentive Plans As Praise and Other Bribes, Houghton Mifflin Company, New York 1999

Laszlo, Ervin, The Systems View of the World: A Holistic Vision for Our Time, Hampton Press Inc., Cresskill, NJ 2002

Lawyer, Edward E. III, Rewarding Excellence: Pay Strategies for the New Economy, Josey-Bass Publishers, San Francisco 2000

McChesney, Chris, Sean Covey and Jim Huling, The 4 Disciplines of Execution, Free Press Simon & Schuster, Inc. New York, NY 2012

O'Connor, Joseph and McDermott, Ian, The Art of Systems Thinking: Essential Skills for Creativity and Problem Solving, Harper Collins, London 1997

Ratey M.D., John J. and Eric Hagerman, Spark: the revolutionary new science of exercise and the brain, Little, Brown and Company, New York 2008

Schwartz M.D., Jeffery M. and Begley, Sharon, The Mind and The Brain: Neuroplasticity and the Power of Mental Force,

Sternberg, Robert J., Handbook of Creativity, Cambridge University Press, United Kingdom 1999

Zaltman, Gerald, How Customers Think: Essential Insights into

the Mind of the Market, Harvard Business School Press, Boston
2003

.